# Beyond the Therapeutic State

The therapeutic state is a pervasive set of practices and ideologies which have been ever present in the twentieth century. This book of international contributions is about bringing into question many of these reified, dogmatic ideologies.

Classifications, diagnosis and the treatments have been shown to be ineffectual for many populations across the globe, but still we persist with redundant, defunct methods and techniques. Why? Because, as some would suggest, we have nothing better. The danger that the state is taking away one of the last confidential spaces for people to allow thoughts to come to them has never been greater.

This book invites readers to think beyond the state and its therapeutics. It will be relevant to many professions, professionals, service users, families, survivors and organisations; and those who are looking for something different. This book was originally published as a special issue of the *European Journal of Psychotherapy & Counselling.*

**Del Loewenthal** is Emeritus Professor of Psychotherapy and Counselling at the University of Roehampton, London, UK. He is an existential-analytic psychotherapist, photographer and chartered psychologist, with a particular interest in phenomenology. His books include *Existential Psychotherapy and Counselling after Postmodernism* (Routledge 2017). www.delloewenthal.com; www.safpac.co.uk.

**Ottar Ness**, PhD, is a family therapist, Professor of Counselling at the Norwegian University of Science and Technology, Professor of Mental Health Care at University College of South-Eastern Norway and Senior Advisor for the National Competence Centre for Mental Healthcare in Norway. His research is in the area of relational welfare in order to co-construct and co-create dignifying lives and communities. He also works with research recovery processes and recovery-oriented practices and services with people with mental health and substance abuse problems. Among his latest books are a handbook of couples therapy, a handbook of family therapy and *Action Research in a Relational Perspective* (Routledge 2019).

**Billy Hardy** is Senior Lecturer in Systemic Psychotherapy at the Family Institute, University of South Wales, UK, and has been course leader for the postgraduate clinical training for many years. He has a professional background in mental health and mental health nursing. He also offers professional consultation to a wide variety of practitioners in the mental health and social care fields.

# Beyond the Therapeutic State

*Edited by*
**Del Loewenthal, Ottar Ness and Billy Hardy**

Routledge
Taylor & Francis Group
LONDON AND NEW YORK

First published 2020
by Routledge
2 Park Square, Milton Park, Abingdon, Oxon, OX14 4RN

and by Routledge
52 Vanderbilt Avenue, New York, NY 10017

*Routledge is an imprint of the Taylor & Francis Group, an informa business*



*British Library Cataloguing in Publication Data*
A catalogue record for this book is available from the British Library

ISBN13: 978-0-367-43662-9

Typeset in Times LT Std
by Newgen Publishing UK

**Publisher's Note**
The publisher accepts responsibility for any inconsistencies that may have arisen during the conversion of this book from journal articles to book chapters, namely the inclusion of journal terminology.

**Disclaimer**
Every effort has been made to contact copyright holders for their permission to reprint material in this book. The publishers would be grateful to hear from any copyright holder who is not here acknowledged and will undertake to rectify any errors or omissions in future editions of this book.

# Contents

# Citation Information

The following chapters in this book were originally published in the *European Journal of Psychotherapy & Counselling*, volume 17, issue 4 (December 2015). When citing this material, please use the original page numbering for each article, as follows:

**Chapter 1**
*The triumph of American psychiatry: How it created the modern therapeutic state*
Robert Whitaker
*European Journal of Psychotherapy & Counselling*, volume 17, issue 4 (December 2015), pp. 326–341

**Chapter 2**
*Children's mental health: Time to stop using psychiatric diagnosis*
Sami Timimi
*European Journal of Psychotherapy & Counselling*, volume 17, issue 4 (December 2015), pp. 342–358

**Chapter 3**
*Psychiatric diagnoses, 'thought styles', and ex post facto fact fallacies*
John Shotter
*European Journal of Psychotherapy & Counselling*, volume 17, issue 4 (December 2015), pp. 359–372

**Chapter 4**
*Radical presence: Alternatives to the therapeutic state*
Sheila McNamee
*European Journal of Psychotherapy & Counselling*, volume 17, issue 4 (December 2015), pp. 373–383

**Chapter 5**
*The extended therapy room*
Carina Håkansson
*European Journal of Psychotherapy & Counselling*, volume 17, issue 4 (December 2015), pp. 384–401

**Chapter 6**

*From victimhood to sisterhood – A practice-based reflexive inquiry into narrative informed group work with women who have experienced sexual abuse*
Leah Salter
*European Journal of Psychotherapy & Counselling,* volume 17, issue 4 (December 2015), pp. 402–417

**Chapter 7**

*Psychotherapy and its alternatives: Commentary on a critique*
Michael Rustin
*European Journal of Psychotherapy & Counselling,* volume 17, issue 4 (December 2015), pp. 418–428

**Chapter 8**

*Dark clouds*
Chris Oakley
*European Journal of Psychotherapy & Counselling,* volume 17, issue 4 (December 2015), pp. 429–440

# Notes on Contributors

**Carina Håkansson** is a licensed psychotherapist and founder of Family Care Foundation in Gothenburg, Sweden, where she was Managing Director until 2015, when she founded The Extended Therapy Room Foundation.

**Billy Hardy** is Senior Lecturer in Systemic Psychotherapy at the Family Institute, University of South Wales, UK.

**Del Loewenthal** is Emeritus Professor of Psychotherapy and Counselling at the University of Roehampton, London, UK.

**Sheila McNamee** is Professor of Communication at the University of New Hampshire and Co-founder and Vice President of the Taos Institute (taosinstitute.net).

**Ottar Ness**, PhD, is a family therapist, Professor of Counselling at the Norwegian University of Science and Technology, Professor of Mental Health Care at University College of South-Eastern Norway and Senior Advisor for the National Competence Centre for Mental Healthcare in Norway.

**Chris Oakley** is a psychoanalyst working in private practice in London, UK.

**Michael Rustin** is Professor in the School of Social Sciences, University of East London, UK.

**Leah Salter** is a UKCP-registered family and systemic psychotherapist based in the UK.

**John Shotter** was Emeritus Professor of Communication in the Department of Communication, University of New Hampshire, USA.

**Sami Timimi** is Visiting Professor of Child Psychiatry and Mental Health Improvement at the University of Lincoln, UK.

**Robert Whitaker** is the author of three books on psychiatry, including *Anatomy of an Epidemic*, which won the US Investigative Reporters and Editors book award for best investigative journalism in 2010.

# Introduction: Beyond the Therapeutic State

Del Loewenthal, Ottar Ness and Billy Hardy

The therapeutic state is a pervasive set of practices and ideologies which are increasingly present in the twenty-first century, controlling our thinking about how we should be in the world. Classifications, diagnoses and treatments have been shown to be ineffectual for many populations across the globe, but still we persist with redundant, defunct methods and techniques. Why? Because, as some would suggest, we have nothing better and others say that they are important as a means of social control.

One danger is that the state is taking away one of the last confidential spaces for people to allow thoughts to come to them, and this danger has never been greater – perhaps George Orwell's '1984' has already been and gone! This book of international contributors is about bringing into question many of these reified, dogmatic ideologies. We see this book as an invitation to think beyond the state and its therapeutics for many professions, professionals, service users, families, survivors and organisations; and many others who are looking for something different. In this book we have been able to bring together key writers who, primarily working out of social constructionist positions in their practices, have been pushing the edges of the therapeutic state and its limitations and constraints. Hence the book's name: *Beyond the Therapeutic State*.

The costs in psychiatric and mental health systems are skyrocketing, and prescriptions for psychotropic drugs written in their millions, coupled with the growth of diagnostic labelling, serves to convince us that it is inside people's minds where their problems reside – not in the society of which we are part. The therapeutic and psychiatric language permeates our culture and society; we hear it in the workplace, in schools and institutions of higher education, in professional sports, debate programmes, TV series and films. Since the 1950s, the promise of a 'pharmaceutical cure' for human problems has implied reduction, perhaps even elimination, of mental illness. However, according to the American journalist and author, Robert Whitaker, the opposite is the case. In *Anatomy of an Epidemic* (2010), Whitaker, a contributor to our book, argues that the widespread use of psychotropic drugs has led to an epidemic of people who are disabled because of mental illness. Moreover, he argues that the percentage of disability increased dramatically in all countries around the world that have promoted widespread use of psychiatric medications.

Whittaker is of course not alone in this position, as this book will hopefully illustrate and illuminate. In June 2014, a group of researchers, practitioners, service users and family members organised a conference around this theme, entitled 'Beyond the Therapeutic State'. It was held in Drammen, Norway at what is now the University of South-Eastern Norway (formerly Buskerud and Vestfold University College). Over 200 participants representing 28 different countries were present. The conference had contributors from a large number of international networks, including the Taos Institute, Centre for Mental Health and Substance Abuse at Buskerud and Vestfold University College, Family Institute Wales, Family Care Foundation Sweden, Helsinki Psychotherapy Institute and Mad in America. This brought together academics, researchers, users, family members, professionals and others who have expertise from direct experience with psychiatric treatment systems. The aim was to promote the visions that go beyond current standardised psychiatric and psychotherapeutic practice and to explore new opportunities. As already mentioned, and central to our approach, we consider that most alternatives to diagnosis and medication today continue to localise the problems within the individual's mind as opposed to the community of which we are a part. We argue that we must look beyond this attitude, moving towards relationally oriented communities and through active participation to change the practices and policies for mental health care. So we have a growing list of diagnoses, an ever-growing army of therapeutic helping professionals, establishment of therapeutic institutions in all areas of society, a thriving market for psychotropic drugs as well as a worldwide epidemic of people who are disabled because of mental disorders. It seems timely to ask who it is that actually benefits from this growing 'therapeutic conditioning', and whether it is time to move beyond the therapeutic state?

The first six chapters in this book are therefore from, and are intended to be representative of, this conference where the Taos Institute and its partners from a social constructionist field of thinking and doing gathered in Drammen, Norway drawing on the global connections and affiliations of the Taos Institute. We believe that the first six chapters represent a moment in Drammen which is important to attempt to share. We are also pleased to then open up this conversation by providing two chapters of critical commentaries, which in different ways engaged with the reported ideas in the conference but are also critical of them. The book concludes with a final chapter calling for the resulting need for, and what might be operationally meant by, critical psychotherapy, psychoanalysis and counselling. From the development of notions of critical psychotherapy in response to growing concerns about the therapeutic state, we provide from another international conference ('Do We Need a Critical Psychotherapy? Exploring Talking Therapies in Neoliberal Society, Freud Museum', June 2015) and resulting organisation (The Critical Psychotherapy Network) some further thoughts on how we might have to rethink the training of psychological therapists, if it's not too late.

Regarding the notion of the 'therapeutic state', Thomas Szasz (1984) might be seen as one of the first, if not the first, to write of this. His radical recommendation was that so-called mental patients should be treated like other people and that psychiatrists should be treated like other professionals. This might initially be seen as the person who is the psychiatrist meeting the person who is the so-called mental health patient. However, his meaning went far beyond this with an aim to disarm psychiatrists, similarly to how 'the Founding Fathers of the United States of America disarmed priests', in order for us all to be free of the detrimental aspects of the therapeutic state. A second book with the same title is by James Nolan. Here in *The Therapeutic State* (1998), Nolan argues that with a steady decline in public confidence the American state has embraced a therapeutic code of moral understanding to legitimise its existence. Hence, the state increasingly turns to the therapeutic ethos as a justification for its policies, leading to the emergence of therapeutic sensibilities in the processes of the American state. Subsequently, in Chriss (1999) the contributors continue this exploration of what they regard as the rise and persistence of the therapeutic welfare state and its guiding concepts including sickness, disease, addiction and self-esteem. They see this as a reflection of the power within a post-industrial society of the professional discourses of medicine, with the assumption of the disease model. By 2017 it was reported that '...much of Nolan's analysis is more pertinent than ever. The therapeutic state, as he saw it in 1998, has now become the norm with therapy and counselling deemed a central state function, writ large in policymakers intensifying focus on mental health' (Nolan, 2017). The question is raised: "is there any scope to resist it?"

In order to attempt to answer this question, this book starts with the aforementioned six chapters which, it is hoped, provide a useful web of ideas from the conference. In chapter one, 'The triumph of American psychiatry: How it created the modern therapeutic state,' Robert Whitaker provides the introduction to his position. He spells out what he sees as some stark realities of the psychiatric system's dilemmas and practices. He focuses not only on the US context but gives a warning of what is currently developing across the globe. He highlights the almost palpable direct consequences of the *DSM* on counselling and psychotherapy practices, along with other therapeutically oriented ways of offering services to help people deal with their distress and problems of living. More specifically, he argues that in the past 170 years, American psychiatry has progressively asserted its authority over a larger segment of the American population. From the mid-1800s to the end of World War II, psychiatry had authority over the asylum population, which markedly increased in the first half of the twentieth century due to the influence of eugenics, an ideology that argued the 'mentally ill' had to be segregated from society. After the war, American psychiatry adopted Freudian conceptions of mental disorders, which enabled it to begin treating people in the community who were 'neurotic' in some way, which dramatically expanded its influence in society. Then, in the 1970s, when many in American society were questioning psychiatry's legitimacy as a branch of medicine, the American Psychiatric Association (APA) responded by adopting a disease model for diagnosing mental disorders, which it set forth in the third edition of its *Diagnostic and Statistical Manual*. There were no scientific discoveries that led to this new model (see, for example, Davies, 2013) but soon the APA was informing the American public that mental disorders were diseases of the brain, and that psychiatric drugs helped fix those diseases, 'like insulin for diabetes'. For Whitaker, the APA, in concert with pharmaceutical companies, has successfully exported this belief system to much of the developed world; and, in order to break free of this 'therapeutic state', the public needs to understand the history of how it came to be, and see the social injury it has caused.

Chapter two, 'Children's mental health: Time to stop using psychiatric diagnosis', is by Sami Timimi. Timimi, author of *Mis-understanding ADHD* (2007), is a psychiatrist and critical thinker of his own field, bringing together the challenge of diagnosis. Thinking from within and beyond the state, he offers us a bold critique of thinking too much from inside the box, and brings the field and science of the psychiatric diagnostic process into question. In this chapter, he offers a critique of how bad evidence can lead to bad thinking and the dangers inherit in that. Timimi suggests that hegemonic mental health service approaches stress the need for 'accurate' diagnosis in order to understand what the correct 'treatment' should be. He reviews the evidence on how far diagnosis in psychiatry has helped advance scientific knowledge and clinical practice and concludes that it hasn't. He then examines how the National Institute for Health and Care Excellence (NICE) guidelines in relation to children's behaviour problems reflect the lack of progress that results from adopting a diagnostic approach. Timimi further argues that taking mental health practice beyond reliance on narrow non-evidence-based diagnostic algorithms can be developed by adopting existing processes such as the Partners for Change Outcome Management Systems project.

Chapter three, 'Psychiatric diagnoses, "thought styles", and ex post facto fact fallacies', is by the late John Shotter who also wrote *Social Construction on the Edge* (2010). Shotter deconstructed for us the diagnostic, and therefore the linguistic, contradictions. He drew upon our use of language to illustrate the pitfalls of not attending to relationship in an attempt to alert us how not to rely on certainty to inform how we relate, communicate and engage with and towards each other. For Shotter, living in two-way, *dialogical* relations with our surroundings, rather than in monological, one-way causal relations with them, means that we can no longer treat ourselves as inquiring simply into a world of objective 'things' already existing in the world around us. We need to see ourselves instead as always acting 'from within', a still-in-process world of flowing streams of intermingling activities affecting us as much, if not more, than we can affect them. In such a world as this, instead of discovering pre-existing things in our inquiries, we continually bring such 'things' into existence. So, although we may talk of discovering certain nameable 'things' in our inquiries, the fact is, we can *only* see such 'things' as *having been at work* in people's activities *after* they have performed them. This, Shotter argued, is also the case with all our diagnostic categories of mental distress – thus to see the 'things' they name as the *causes* of a person's distress is to commit an ex post facto fact fallacy. Something else altogether 'moves' people in the performance of their actions than the nameable 'things' we currently claim to have discovered in our inquiries.

Sheila McNamee is the author of chapter four: 'Radical presence: Alternatives to the therapeutic state' and co-author, with Kenneth Gergen, of *Relational Responsibility* (1998). McNamee continues the theme of previous authors and offers us challenging and provoking ideas. She invites us to consider how we can position ourselves in relation to others and the dominant discourse which shapes and constrains us. McNamee introduces the idea of radical presence as an alternative to the current therapeutic state (or psy-complex) within which we live today. For McNamee, radical presence challenges us to confront the dominance of psychological discourses which define, control and limit the ways in which we live. It shifts our attention from diagnosis and treatment of individuals to an exploration of broader relational and institutional contexts, and the ways in which professionals and ordinary people alike can be responsive, present and open to a multiplicity of life forms.

This leads to the final two chapters in this part of the book, and opens a window to practices which challenge the therapeutic state and its current paraphernalia for constraint and control. Carina Håkansson, author of chapter five, 'The extended therapy room' and of *Ordinary Life Therapy* (2009), provides us with a snapshot of her practices in a Swedish context. As a key presentation at the conference, she brought to life the therapeutic work she does with families beyond the therapy room and beyond the therapeutic state. In this chapter, she illustrates her approach by inviting us into her way of working in and with relational practices. For Håkansson, the Family Care Foundation was created in 1987 as a reaction to a system which far too often seems to forget it is real people involved, both those called clients and professional helpers. She suggests that it is as if knowledge from ordinary life often is put aside when entering a professional context. Manuals and specific methods have increased steadily over the years, as has psychiatric diagnosis and prescription of pharmaceuticals. Håkansson argues that regardless of whether we are called therapists, family homes or clients, we are affected by each other and the situations we find ourselves in. We bear with us our personal history while we are also part of a larger context. She considers that those of us working as psychotherapists have a potential to contribute with knowledge regarding human beings and human life conditions. Håkansson then describes and discusses some central themes found in practice and through research. She argues that in psychotherapy, as in life, there are moments and situations that can't be proven or verbally explained, and which perhaps can't be completely understood. For Håkansson, our shared work in the Extended Therapy Room entails, as in life, moments of deepest fear as well as moments of wonderful joy. Håkansson has now founded 'The Extended Therapy Room Foundation'. She is also co-founder of the International Institute for Psychiatric Drug Withdrawal (IIPDW).

Chapter six, 'From victimhood to sisterhood – A practice-based reflexive inquiry into narrative informed group work with women who have experienced sexual abuse', is by Leah Salter. Salter offers a glimpse into the world of shaping experiences with clients, to moving in and between the various positions as researcher, therapist researcher, collaborator and researcher participant. She illuminates the shifting of these positions into being one of a group coordinating therapeutic, helpful and sustainable service without the state to aid this. In this chapter, Salter's aims are to present some of the relational contexts and considerations of a female therapist's role within an island community group for women who have shared experiences of abuse and injustice; her relationship to the group; to her systemic and narrative practices; and to the research that has ensued. Salter explores the changing relational contexts as the group moves from a facilitator-led to a peer support group; and the associated language shifts from a binary discourse of 'other than' to a collective definition of 'sisterhood'. She argues that this is part of the story, which also includes the important themes of community engagement, social action and the complexities of insider/practice-based research.

Our next contributions are from invited published respondents to the previous six chapters. In chapter seven, 'Psychotherapy and its alternatives: Commentary on a critique', Michael Rustin, whose writings about psychoanalysis, society and politics have more recently focused on the harmful consequences of neoliberalism (*After Neoliberalism: The Kilburn Manifesto*, 2015), reviews the preceding six chapters outlining their main aims and arguments. He provides some critical reflections, asking questions about the key concept of the 'therapeutic state'. Rustin notes that little attention is given to psychoanalytic or other psychological theories of the mind, as distinct from the biological models which are the main object of criticism in the preceding chapters. He argues that just as it is justifiable and useful to take account of theories of the mind in considering issues of mental health and therapy, so it is desirable also to take account of the structures of society which have responsibility for generating conditions of mental well- or ill-being, and to reflect on how these may be changed. Rustin argues that the counter-cultural and somewhat 'post-modern' critical approach which informs the preceding conference chapters can only form part of a sufficient response to the problems which the conference identifies.

Chapter eight, 'Dark clouds', is by our second invited published respondent, Chris Oakley, a psychoanalyst who was involved with the RD Laing/David Cooper 'anti-psychiatry' initiatives and author of *Football Delirium* (2007). He considers this chapter to be in part a response to this book's first six chapters from the Norway conference and he utilises these as a springboard to expand certain ideas regarding the history and the terrain concerning the mental health issues in our culture. From this, Oakley proposes that there is a fundamental unrelenting tension between two polarities: one reactionary and authoritarian, fixated on a concern with outcomes, propped up by closed systems of thought, managerial, habitually linked to adaptation and conformity; the other more romantically seen as revolutionary, un-handcuffing madness from mental illness, facilitating more expansive, freewheeling possibilities within all our lives. For Oakley, much of this pays tribute to some of the major figures in the history of 'anti-psychiatry' (Basaglia, Cooper and Laing), with the costs involved. Oakley traces out the genesis and consequences of what he considers to be the two predominant 'clouds' permeating our world, the paranoid and the digital, which he argues are all converging on 'a naturalisation of our culture of surveillance, and an insistence on control. Otherwise known as a culture of fear'.

Finally, chapter nine, 'Altermodernity and the unfortunate need to train critical psychotherapists and counsellors', is by Del Loewenthal, whose books include *Critical Psychotherapy, Psychoanalysis and Counselling: Implications for Practice* (2015). Loewenthal argues that critical psychotherapy, psychoanalysis and counselling is a response to the increasing concern about growing state influences on the talking therapies, where the longstanding pressures on psychiatry and psychology to be agents of the state are now increasingly being applied to psychotherapy, psychoanalysis and counselling. Loewenthal considers the problems that have led to a need for critical psychotherapy and counselling together with some of their implications for the training of psychological therapists, if not psycho-social or community therapists, so that instead of increasingly becoming part of the problem of the therapeutic state we could become part of its antidote.

The chapters in this volume represent the contributors' ongoing thinking and practice as counsellors and psychotherapists, practitioners, academics and researchers across a variety of countries and boundaries, whether physical or political (which continues to evolve; see for example, Morrill, 2019). We hope that the ideas presented will stimulate and energise other ways of thinking about our ongoing practices and lead to new connections and social constructionist positions. We see this book as an invitation to think beyond the state and its therapeutics for many professions, professionals, service users, families, survivors and organisations; and many others who are looking for something different.

## References

Chriss, J. (1999). *Counseling and the therapeutic state*. New York: Aldine de Gruyter.

Davies, J. (2013). *Cracked: The unhappy truth about psychiatry*. London: Icon Books.

Håkansson, C. (2009). *Ordinary life therapy*. Chagrin Falls, OH: Taos.

McNamee, S., & Gergen, K. J. (Eds.). (1998). *Relational responsibility*. London: Sage.

Loewenthal, D. (2015). *Critical psychotherapy, psychoanalysis and counselling: Implications for practice*. Basingstoke: Palgrave Macmillan.

Morrill, Z. (2019, July 1). 'UN report criticizes biomedical approach to mental health'. *Mad in America*. Retrieved from www.madinamerica.com/2019/07/un-report-criticizes-biomedical-approach-mental-health/

Nolan, J. (1998). *The therapeutic state*. Princeton, NJ: Princeton University Press.

Nolan, J. L. Jr. (2017, 1 September). On the therapeutic state. *Spiked*. Retrieved from www.spiked-online.com/2017/09/01/on-the-therapeutic-state/

Oakley, C. (2007). *Football delirium*. London: Routledge.

Orwell, G. (2004). *Nineteen eighty-four*. London: Penguin Books Ltd.

Rustin, M., Hall, S., & Massey, D. (2015). *After neoliberalism: The Kilburn manifesto*. London: Lawrence and Wishart Ltd.

Shotter, J. (2010). *Social construction on the edge, witness-thinking and embodiment*. Chagrin Falls, OH: Taos.

Szasz, T (1984). *The therapeutic state: Psychiatry in the mirror of current events*. Buffalo, NY: Prometheus Books.

Timimi, S. (2007).*Mis-understanding ADHD: The complete guide for parents to alternatives to drugs*. Bloomington, IN: Author House.

Whitaker, R. (2010). *Anatomy of an epidemic*. New York: Broadway Paperbacks.

# The triumph of American psychiatry: How it created the modern therapeutic state

Robert Whitaker

Over the past 170 years, American psychiatry has progressively asserted its authority over a larger segment of the American population. From the mid-1800s to the end of World War II, psychiatry had authority over the asylum population, which markedly increased in the first half of the twentieth century due to the influence of eugenics, an ideology that argued the 'mentally ill' had to be segregated from society. After the war, American psychiatry adopted Freudian conceptions of mental disorders, which enabled it to begin treating people in the community who were 'neurotic' in some way, which dramatically expanded its influence in society. Then, in the 1970s, when many in American society were questioning psychiatry's legitimacy as a branch of medicine, the American Psychiatric Association (APA) responded by adopting a disease model for diagnosing mental disorders, which it set forth in the third edition of its Diagnostic and Statistical Manual. There were no scientific discoveries that led to this new model, but soon the APA was informing the American public that mental disorders were diseases of the brain, and that psychiatric drugs helped fix those diseases, 'like insulin for diabetes.' The APA, in concert with pharmaceutical companies, has successfully exported this belief system to much of the developed world. In order to break free of this 'therapeutic state,' the public needs to understand the history of how it came to be, and see the social injury it has caused.

Innerhalb der letzten 170 Jahre konnte die amerikanische Psychiatrie ihren Einfluss auf immer breitere Teile der amerikanischen Bevölkerung ausweiten. Von Mitte des 18. Jahrhunderts bis zum Ende des Zweiten Weltkriegs war die Psychiatrie vor allem für Asylsuchende zuständig. Der Einflussbereich konnte jedoch in der ersten Hälfte des 20. Jahrhunderts, durch die zunehmende Popularität der Eugenik-Ideologie, und deren Ziel, psychisch Kranke von der Gesellschaft auszuschließen, noch mal deutlich ausgeweitet werden. Nach dem Krieg übernahm die amerikanische Psychiatrie dann einige Konzepte der Freudschen Psychoanalyse, die es ihr ermöglichte, Personen, die in gewisser Weise "neurotisch" waren, innerhalb des Gemeinwesens zu behandeln. Dies dehnte den Einflussbereich innerhalb der Gesellschaft massiv aus. In den 1970ern schließlich, als viele Amerikaner die Legitimität der Psychiatrie als einen Zweig der Medizin infrage stellten, führte die amerikanische Psychiatrievereinigung (APA) ein Modell ein, um psychische Krankheiten zu diagnostizieren. Dieses Diagnosemodell wurde in die damals dritte Auflage des diagnostischen und statistischen Leitfadens für psychische Störungen aufgenommen. Es gab keinerlei wissenschaftliche Untersuchungen, die dieses neue Modell stützten. Dennoch ging die APA relativ bald dazu über, die amerikanische Öffentlichkeit darüber in Kenntnis zu setzen, dass psychische Störungen Krankheiten des Gehirns sind, und dass Psychopharmaka helfen, dieses Leiden zu beheben – gleichsam wie "Insulin für Diabetiker". Die APA hat diesen Glauben, im Zusammenspiel mit der Pharmaindustrie, erfolgreich in weiten Teilen der Welt verbreitet. Um diese "Therapiegesellschaft" zu überwinden, muss die Öffentlichkeit die Entstehungsgeschichte verstehen, muss gezeigt werden, wie es dazu kam und welchen gesellschaftlichen Schaden es angerichtet hat.

En los últimos ciento setenta años la psiquiatría americana ha reafirmado progresivamente su autoridad sobre una gran parte de la población americana. Desde mediados de 1800 hasta el final de la segunda guerra mundial, la psiquiatría tuvo autoridad sobre los pacientes recluidos en asilos, la cual aumentó mucho durante la primera mitad del siglo XX debido a la influencia de la eugenesia, una ideología que proponía que las personas mentalmente enfermas debían ser segregadas de la sociedad. Después de la guerra, la psiquiatría americana adoptó las concepciones freudianas acerca de los trastornos mentales, lo cual le permitió comenzar a tratar en la comunidad las personas que eran ''neuróticas'' de alguna manera, esto extendió dramáticamente su influencia en la sociedad. Luego, en los años setenta, cuando muchos dentro de la sociedad americana cuestionaban la legitimidad de la psiquiatría como una rama de la medicina, la Asociación Psiquiátrica Americana (APA) respondió adoptando un modelo de enfermedad para diagnosticar los trastornos mentales, el cual salió a la luz en la tercera edición de su llamado Manual de Diagnóstico y Estadísticas (DSM). Ningún descubrimiento científico apoyó este nuevo modelo, pero muy pronto la APA informó al público americano que los trastornos mentales eran enfermedades del cerebro y que las drogas psiquiátricas ayudaban a mejorarlos ''tal como lo hacía la insulina con la diabetes'. La APA, en coordinación con las compañías farmacéuticas, ha exportado exitosamente este sistema de creencias hacia la mayor parte del mundo. Para liberarnos de este ''estado terapéutico'', el público necesita conocer y entender la historia de lo que ha sucedido y ver realmente el gran daño social que ha causado.

Nel corso degli ultimi 170 anni, la psichiatria americana ha progressivamente affermato la sua autorità su un ampio sezione della popolazione americana. Dalla metà del 1800 fino alla fine della seconda guerra mondiale, la psichiatria aveva potere sulla popolazione protetta, esso è notevolmente aumentato nella prima metà del 20° secolo a causa dell'influenza dell'eugenetica, un'ideologia che ha sostenuto che il "malato di mente" dovesse essere segregato dalla società. Dopo la guerra, la psichiatria americana ha adottato i concetti freudiani relativi ai disturbi mentali, il che le ha consentito di iniziare a trattare soggetti in qualche modo "nevrotici" nella comunità, e che ha ampliato notevolmente la sua influenza nella società. Successivamente, nel 1970, quando molti nella società americana si stavano interrogando circa la legittimità della psichiatria come branca della medicina, l'American Psychiatric Association (APA) ha reagito adottando un modello per la diagnosi dei disturbi mentali, che è esposto nella terza edizione del Diagnostic and Statistical Manual (DSM). Non sono state le scoperte scientifiche a portare a questo modello, piuttosto l'APA ha istruito l'opinione pubblica americana sui disordini mentali considerati malattie del cervello e curabili con i farmaci così "come l'insulina per il diabete". L'APA, in concerto con le aziende farmaceutiche, ha esportato con successo questo sistema di credenze a buona parte del mondo sviluppato. Per liberarsi di questo "stato terapeutico", il pubblico ha bisogno di comprendere la storia di quanto è avvenuto e vederne il danno sociale causato.

Au cours des 170 dernières années, la psychiatrie américaine a progressivement assis son autorité sur un large segment de la population américaine. Depuis le milieu du 19ieme siècle jusqu'à la fin de la deuxième guerre mondiale, la psychiatrie avait autorité sur la population asilaire, qui a augmenté de manière significative dans la première moitié du 20ieme siècle sous l'influence de l'eugénisme, une idéologie prônant que les 'malades mentaux 'devaient être tenus à l'écart de la société. Après la guerre, la psychiatrie américaine adopta les conceptions freudiennes de désordres mentaux, ce qui lui permit de traiter les gens en ambulatoire qui étaient 'névrosés' d'une certaine manière, ce qui favorisa l'expansion de son influence dans la société. Puis, dans les années 70, alors que beaucoup dans la société américaine questionnaient la légitimité de la psychiatrie en tant que branche de la médecine, l'Association Américaine de Psychiatrie (APA) répondit en adoptant un modèle de la maladie pour diagnostiquer les désordres psychiques, énoncés dans la troisième édition de son DSM (Diagnostic and Statistical Manual). Il n'y avait pas eu de découvertes scientifiques conduisant à la mise en place de ce nouveau modèle, mais bientôt l'APA informait le public américain que les maladies mentales étaient des maladies du cerveau et que les drogues psychiatriques soignaient ces maladies, 'comme l'insuline le diabète'. L'APA, de concert avec les compagnies pharmaceutiques, a exporté avec succès ce système de croyance vers la plupart du monde développé. Pour se libérer de cet 'Etat thérapeutique' le public doit comprendre l'histoire de son émergence et réaliser le préjudice social causé.

Κατά τα τελευταία 170 χρόνια, η αμερικανική ψυχιατρική έχει κυριαρχήσει σταδιακά σε ένα μεγάλο τμήμα του αμερικανικού πληθυσμού. Από τα μέσα της δεκαετίας του 1800 μέχρι το τέλος του Β' Παγκοσμίου Πολέμου, η ψυχιατρική ασκούσε εξουσία στον πληθυσμό των ασύλων, ο οποίος αυξήθηκε σημαντικά κατά το πρώτο μισό του 20ου αιώνα, λόγω της επίδρασης της ευγονικής, μιας ιδεολογίας που υποστήριζε ότι οι «ψυχικά ασθενείς» έπρεπε να απομονώνονται από την υπόλοιπη κοινωνία. Μετά τον πόλεμο, η αμερικανική ψυχιατρική υιοθέτησε τη φροϋδική αντίληψη για τις ψυχικές διαταραχές, κάτι που της επέτρεψε να ξεκινήσει να θεραπεύει ανθρώπους στην κοινότητα που ήταν «νευρωτικοί», κατά κάποιο τρόπο, ενισχύοντας με τον τρόπο αυτό δραματικά την επιρροή που είχε στην κοινωνία. Στη συνέχεια, στη δεκαετία του 1970, όταν πολλοί στην αμερικανική κοινωνία αμφισβητούσαν τη νομιμότητα της ψυχιατρικής ως κλάδου της ιατρικής, η Αμερικανική Ψυχιατρική Εταιρεία (APA) αντέδρασε υιοθετώντας ένα ιατρικό μοντέλο που βασίζεται στην έννοια της νόσου για τη διάγνωση ψυχικών διαταραχών, το οποίο διατυπώθηκε στην τρίτη έκδοση του Διαγνωστικού και Στατιστικού Εγχειριδίου (DSM). Παρόλο που δεν υπήρξαν επιστημονικές ανακαλύψεις που οδήγησαν σε αυτό το νέο μοντέλο, η APA σύντομα διέδωσε την πληροφορία στην αμερικανική κοινή γνώμη ότι οι ψυχικές διαταραχές είναι ασθένειες του εγκεφάλου, και ότι τα ψυχιατρικά φάρμακα βοηθούν στην καταπολέμησή τους, «όπως η ινσουλίνη για τον διαβήτη». Η APA, σε συνεργασία με τις φαρμακευτικές εταιρείες, έχει προωθήσει με επιτυχία αυτό το σύστημα πεποιθήσεων σε ένα μεγάλο μέρος του ανεπτυγμένου κόσμου. Προκειμένου να απελευθερωθεί από αυτή τη «θεραπευτικό κράτος», το κοινό χρειάζεται να κατανοήσει την ιστορία της πορείας της μέχρι σήμερα, και να αναγνωρίσει τη βλάβη σε κοινωνικό επίπεδο που έχει προκαλέσει.

## Introduction

My first thought when I was invited to speak at a 2014 conference in Norway titled 'Beyond the Therapeutic State' was of the remarkable increase in psychiatry's authority in the United States during the past 35 years, and how American society has indeed become a therapeutic state. The profession has asserted a medical expertise over all ages, from the very young to the elderly. My second thought was of the witty title of a 1993 book, which cast a suspicious eye on a wider group of professionals: *We've Had a Hundred Years of Psychotherapy and the World's Getting Worse* (Hillman & Ventura, 1993).

It is American psychiatry, though, that has created the 'therapeutic state.' The American Psychiatric Association (APA), through its *Diagnostic and Statistical Manual (DSM)*, has set forth conceptions of 'mental illness' that ensnare an ever-larger percentage of the population into the 'patient' category, and also popularized these diagnoses, such that the American public is constantly on the lookout for signs of mental illness in themselves and others (American Psychiatric Association [APA], 1980, 1994, 2013; Whitaker & Cosgrove, 2015). Children born into this therapeutic state are regularly diagnosed with ADHD, depression, and bipolar disorder. Although it is hard to get current data on this diagnostic tsunami, a recent study found that 11% of our school-age children have been diagnosed with ADHD alone (Visser et al., 2014). As for the general population, more than 20% of American adults take a psychiatric drug on a daily basis, and there are many others who, while eschewing psychiatric drugs, pay for psychotherapy or other types of counseling (Medco, 2011).

The APA, in concert with the pharmaceutical industry, has also succeeded in exporting this 'therapeutic state' to much of Europe and the rest of the developed world. It can be likened to the spread of a belief system, and in order to explore how to 'move beyond' it, it is helpful to understand how it came to be, and the social injury it is causing.

### *The birth of the therapeutic state*

Conventional histories of psychiatry regularly tell of how, prior to 1955, the field lacked effective treatments for mental disorders, and then the antipsychotic chlorpromazine was discovered, and this ushered in a 'psychopharmacological revolution,' which produced a great advance in care (Shorter, 1997). But one of the surprises to be found by digging through the history books is that early on in the United States, there was a period when a non-therapeutic approach, promoted by the Quakers, was the preferred treatment of the day, which arguably produced outcomes much superior to outcomes for 'mad' patients today (Bockoven, 1972; Dain, 1964; Grob, 1973, 1994; Scull, 1989; Whitaker, 2002).

Known as 'moral therapy,' it was developed by Quakers in York, England in response to the harsh medical therapeutics of the day. In eighteenth-century England, 'doctors' ran madhouses for the insane, where they regularly employed somatic therapies designed to weaken and subdue the mad. The thought was that the mad, by virtue of having lost their reason, had descended to a lower level of being, and medical texts of the day advocated the use of 'therapies' meant to 'tame' their animal-like behaviors (Cullen, 1805; Hunter, 1963; Morton, 1895; Rush, 1812/1962; Scull, 1989; Zilboorg, 1941). In 1796, Quakers in York, upset that one of their members had died in a madhouse of ill treatment and neglect, opened a small 'retreat' in the countryside. Instead of thinking of the mad as less than human, the Quakers conceived of them as 'brethren' who should be provided with good shelter and food, and treated with kindness. In this way, the Quakers hoped that they could 'assist nature' in helping their insane brethren get well. Their belief was that the mad had an inner, God-given capacity to regain self-control and recover their reason (Tuke, 1813).

This was a decidedly non-medical approach, and starting in 1817, Quakers in the United States began opening such retreats in Philadelphia, New York City, and Boston. Just as the Quakers in York distrusted the 'mad doctors,' so did the American Quakers (Grob, 1973; Scull, 1989; Whitaker, 2002). As one early asylum director in the United States remarked, he 'and his colleagues were so prejudiced against the use of medical measures, as to object even to the election of physicians in their board, being fearful they might effect some innovation' (Dain, 1964).

However, with the Quakers opening such retreats, it was clear that an age of 'asylum-building' had begun in the United States, and local medical societies understood that they were going to lose authority over the 'mad' if this Quaker-led movement continued. The Connecticut Medical Society, sizing up this threat, lobbied state and civic groups to build a local asylum, one that would mostly follow the Quaker model, but with this exception: it would be led by a physician (Scull, 1989).

When the Hartford Retreat in Connecticut opened in 1824, superintendent Dr Eli Todd noted that it would provide *both* medical treatments and the environmental therapy of the Quakers to the insane, and argued that this combination should lead to superior outcomes (Scull, 1989). This became the new model for asylums in the United States, and as a result, asylum medicine was on its way to becoming its own specialty. In 1844, superintendents at 13 asylums formed the Association of Medical Superintendents of American Institutions for the Insane (AMSAII) to promote their interests, and as a first order of business, they passed a resolution stating that an asylum should always have a physician as its chief executive officer and superintendent (Grob, 1994; Scull, 1989).

There was now a medical group asserting its authority over a segment of the American population – those it would deem insane and in need of hospitalization. Thus was the seed for the rise of a therapeutic state planted, with AMSAII renamed the American Medico-Psychological Association in 1892, and then the APA in 1921 (Shorter, 1997).

### *The growth of the therapeutic state*

In the 1840s, Dorothea Dix – a schoolteacher who had been nursed back to health by Quakers in York, England after suffering a breakdown – began lobbying state governments to build publicly funded moral therapy asylums. The first small retreats had been privately run, and Dix sought to bring this humanitarian care to a larger segment of the American population. State legislatures responded by authorizing the construction of dozens of new mental hospitals. (Dix, 1843). This was the first great public works project in the United States, and quickly the mental hospital became a fixture of the societal landscape in the United States. In 1840, there were only 18 private and public asylums in the United States, with a total census of 2561 patients. Forty years later, there were 139 mental hospitals in the country, with a census of 31,793 people (Deutsch, 1937; Tomes, 1994).

While Dix's intentions were laudable, once the public hospitals were built, communities began dumping all sorts of people into the institutions – the mad, the demented elderly, and others with neurological diseases – and the hospitals quickly grew in size, and were filled to the brim with many patients who had no possibility of recovering. Moral therapy came to be seen as a failed therapy, and the memory of its earlier success, when more than 50% of the newly insane were discharged within a year, was purged from psychiatry's institutional memory (Bockoven, 1972; Dain, 1964; Grob, 1973, 1994; Morton, 1895; Scull, 1989). Psychiatry in the twentieth century would focus on 'scientific,' somatic treatments for the insane.

It was at that time, just before the turn of the century, that the United States began to fall under the spell of eugenic ideas, which led to a further growth of the therapeutic state. Although eugenic ideas were first advanced by England's Sir Francis Galton, the United States was the first nation to incorporate such concepts into social policy and law. In his writings, Galton argued that if a society wanted to remain strong, it had to encourage those with good 'germ plasm' to breed, and prevent those with poor 'germ plasm' from doing so. In order to achieve this goal, a society needed to start grading its citizens, separating the well-born from the poorly born. In the United States, the ruling elite, which was composed of white Anglo Saxons, knew where to find the 'poorly born': there were sure to be many among the blacks newly freed from slavery and the multitudes of immigrants pouring into the country (Kevles, 1985).

In 1896, Connecticut became the first state to enact a law prohibiting the 'insane' from marrying, with the thought that this would prevent them from passing on their bad germ plasm. However, American eugenicists lamented that such laws were ineffective, as few people, when seeking a license to marry, declared that they were 'insane.' As such, eugenicists began arguing that the 'poorly born' needed to be segregated from society, at least during their breeding years, and with some of America's richest men – Andrew Carnegie, John D. Rockefeller, and others – providing the funding to promote these ideas, states began locking up an ever-greater number of people in state mental hospitals, and keeping them there *indefinitely* (Chase, 1980; Mehler, 1988).

This was done without any due process. Whereas those charged with crimes in the United States had a Constitutional right to a fair trial, those deemed mentally ill could be put into a mental hospital against their wishes, and once that occurred, they had no way to challenge this abridgement of their freedom. But it was being done under the province of medical care, which is a signature element of a therapeutic state: the authority and power that is being exercised is often hidden to the public.

With eugenic ideas being embraced by a majority of Americans, the number of people in America's mental hospitals jumped from 31,973 people in 1880 to 419,374 patients in 1940 (Grob, 1983; Myerson, 1936). Along the way, the US Supreme Court authorized the forced sterilization of the mentally ill. This was another example of the expansion of the therapeutic state, and by the end of World War II, 21,311 patients in America's mental institutions had suffered this fate (Robitscher, 1973).

***Expanding into the community***

At the end of World War II, with eugenics becoming discredited because of its association with Nazi Germany, American society suddenly saw a need to hospitalize fewer people. The therapeutic state took a step back, and starting in the early 1950s, many states began talking about discharging patients into the community (even before the arrival of chlorpromazine) (Johnson, 1990). In 1963, John F. Kennedy set forth a plan for deinstitutionalization, and thus America decided, at least in theory, that it would no longer be a society where the mentally ill could be locked up in hospitals for years and years without end (Joint Commission on Mental Illness and Mental Health, 1961).

In a sense, deinstitutionalization could have marked an end to the 'therapeutic state' that had arisen with the building of mental hospitals in the nineteenth century. However, after World War II, a therapeutic enterprise based in the *community* developed in American society, and this ultimately led to the therapeutic state we know today.

At the start of World War II, more than two-thirds of the APA's 2300 members worked in mental hospitals (Grob, 1991). This was the domain of American life that the profession had authority over, as 'talk therapy' had yet to really arrive in American society. Psychiatrists took care of the 'seriously' mentally ill, with the disorders considered to be mostly biological in kind.

However, during the war, psychiatrists assigned to neuropsychiatric units treated soldiers traumatized by battle. In that setting, psychiatrists discovered that 'psychotherapy' plus rest often worked miracles, with 60% of soldiers returning to duty within five days. Psychiatrists now had the experience of seeing ordinary people descend into disturbed states and get better quickly. 'Our experiences with therapy in war neuroses have left us with an optimistic attitude,' wrote psychiatrist Roy Grinker. 'The lessons we have learned in the combat zone can well be applied in rehabilitation at home' (Grob, 1991).

This wartime experience prompted psychiatry to reconsider the nature of mental disorders. Clearly, environmental stresses and other psychological challenges could trigger symptoms of mental illness. This conception fit with Freudian theories, which were popularized after the war, mostly by Jewish psychoanalysts who immigrated to the United States. American psychiatry now saw a way out of the asylum and into the community: they could begin treating people who were not so ill they needed to be hospitalized, but rather were suffering from anxiety and other neurotic conditions (Grob, 1991; Shorter, 1997; Strand, 2011).

With psychiatry expanding it horizons, the number of medical students who chose this specialty soared, and by 1956, the APA had 10,000 members, with the vast majority – 83% – working outside the mental hospital (Grob, 1991). The couch was now the new symbol of the working psychiatrist.

Even as psychiatry was transformed in this way, psychologists stepped into this new marketplace for therapeutic services. Prior to World War II, psychologists mostly focused on developing mental tests and studying the human personality. But after the war ended, psychologists began providing clinical services as well, and their move into the psychotherapy market accelerated in

1951, after Carl Rogers published *Client-Centered Therapy* (Buchanan, 2003; Rogers, 1951).

The number of non-physician therapists in the United States exploded during the next three decades. By 1980, there were 50,000 psychologists in the United States, along with tens of thousands of social workers, family therapists and marriage counselors, all offering help to America's walking wounded (Mayes, 2005). A therapeutic marketplace had sprung up in the United States, and then the APA, in a stroke of commercial genius, published the manual that has so changed American society.

### *DSM III: the medicalization of the American mind*

During the 1970s, the APA found reason to worry about psychiatry's place in society, as critics questioned its legitimacy and utility. Thomas Szasz, Erving Goffman, David Cooper, and others wrote 'antipsychiatry' tracts, arguing that psychiatry functioned more as an agency of social control than as a medical specialty. Ex-patients, upon leaving the hospital, began organizing, dubbing themselves 'survivors of psychiatry.' Together, the academics and ex-patients were challenging psychiatry's authority over the severely mentally ill, and as for its authority over the walking-wounded, researchers were finding that its preferred brand of talk therapy – psychoanalysis – was no more effective than any of the many other types of psychotherapy that were being offered. Furthermore, its diagnoses were ridiculed as highly unreliable. Together, all of these challenges led psychiatry to see itself as a field under siege, threatened – as one leading psychiatrist said – with 'extinction' (Buchanan, 2003; Hackett, 1977; Wilson, 1993).

The APA responded to this crisis by opting to develop a new diagnostic manual. The stated scientific goal was to produce a manual that would improve diagnostic reliability, but, once the remaking of the DSM was underway, it was also evident that guild influences were at play. How could psychiatry repair its public image? How could psychiatry gain a competitive advantage in the psychotherapy marketplace?

An obvious answer beckoned. Psychiatrists were *doctors*, and if they wanted to repair their image with the public, they could emphasize this fact. Instead of presenting themselves as 'shrinks' who listened to patients stretched out on a Freudian couch, they could present themselves as physicians clad in white coats that treated diseases of the brain. In addition, by adopting a 'disease' model for diagnosing mental disorders, it could be expected that drugs would become first-line treatments even for common problems like anxiety, and it was only doctors – and not psychologists, social workers, or counselors – who had prescribing privileges (Buchanan, 2003; Decker, 2013; Mayes, 2005; Strand, 2011; Whitaker & Cosgrove, 2015; Wilson, 1993).

The APA published the third edition of its *Diagnostic and Statistical Manual (DSM III)* in 1980. The manual, which was created under the leadership of Robert Spitzer, listed 265 disorders, and as the APA presented it to the public, it emphasized that psychiatric disorders were to be considered diseases of the brain, 'just as diabetes, heart disease, and cancer are' (Andreasen, 1984;

Whitaker & Cosgrove, 2015). The APA, with funding from the pharmaceutical industry, then ramped up its capacity to tell this story to the public, running media-training courses for its members, sponsoring seminars for the press where it told of 'new advances in psychiatry,' and distributing 'Fact Sheets' that told of the prevalence of mental illnesses listed in *DSM III* and the effectiveness of psychiatric treatments (Whitaker & Cosgrove, 2015).

There had been no scientific discoveries that had led to the creation of DSM III and the APA's adoption of a disease model. Spitzer and his collaborators, as they constructed the boundaries of the 265 disorders, did so with the thought that the manual should be able to provide a diagnosis for everybody who came to a psychiatrist seeking help, as a diagnosis would be essential for insurance reimbursement (Decker, 2013; Mayes, 2005; Strand, 2011). Yet, when the APA presented its disease model to the public, it told of great discoveries having been made, and soon the American public was being told that depression, schizophrenia, and other psychiatric disorders were due to known chemical imbalances in the brain, with psychiatric drugs correcting these imbalances, much like 'insulin for diabetes' (APA, 2005; Andreasen, 1984; Harding, 2001; Lacasse & Leo, 2005; Stotland, 2001; Weiden, 1999; Whitaker & Cosgrove, 2015). This was 'news' that told of an extraordinary medical advance. The pathology of major mental disorders had been discovered, and psychiatry had antidotes for them.

This was the storytelling that remade the American mind, and created the modern therapeutic state, which now governs our lives. Subsequent editions of the DSM–*DSM IV* and *DSM 5* – have simply expanded upon the 'revolution' wrought by *DSM III*, and further expanded the reach of the therapeutic state, with expanded boundaries for the diagnosing of mental disorders in children and adults (APA, 1994, 2013; Caplan, 1995; Frances, 2013; Greenberg, 2013; Horwitz, 2002; Horwitz & Wakefield, 2007; Whitaker & Cosgrove, 2015). The three-year-old who throws tantrums is a candidate for a diagnosis of oppositional defiant disorder. The six-year-old who fidgets too much in the classroom is not a child bored by his or her environment, but rather is suffering from a brain abnormality: attention deficit hyperactivity disorder. The moody teenager may now be diagnosed with depression or bipolar disorder. The adult who feels anxious may be suffering from panic disorder, or general anxiety disorder, or PTSD, or social anxiety disorder, and prescribed an SSRI antidepressant for this ailment. And so on. Those so diagnosed have also been led to understand that their brain chemicals are amiss. This is why they behave like they do, or experience difficult emotions, and this is why they may need to take psychiatric drugs for life.

American society has organized itself around this narrative, with the powers of the 'state' marshaled to promote it too. Schoolteachers have been trained to recognize ADHD in their students, and the federal government provides additional financial support to schools so they can better serve children with this brain disability (Frontline, 2001) Insurance companies readily reimburse for drug treatments for such disorders, while curbing payments for psychotherapy (Harris, 2011). The federal government funds research into these brain disorders, and has prepared materials, for distribution in doctors' office and on the Internet, that tell of brain diseases and chemical imbalances, and of how more than 25% of the American public suffer from a mental illness each year (Bagalman & Napili, 2015). Newspapers and magazines also tell of advances in psychiatric research, diagnosis, and treatment. The public understood this was a story of science, and in this new therapeutic society, dissenting voices found it difficult to find a mainstream forum for their thoughts, as they were dismissed – by the APA and other promoters of this story – as non-scientific, or more colorfully, as 'flat-earthers' (Gorman, 1994).

### *The social injury*

It would require a book-length treatise to detail all the harm that the 'therapeutic state' is doing to American society. In this modern era, the burden of mental illness has exploded, and American children are so conditioned to think of themselves as mentally ill that at many universities, 50% or so of the students access psychiatric services during their four years at school. But if there is one overriding harm, it is that the therapeutic state has instilled in society an impoverished philosophy of being.

The *DSM* appears to be a book authored by people who have never read a novel, or ever attended the theater to witness a Shakespearean play. In the *DSM* world, there is no sense of who we humans are: that we struggle with our minds, that we struggle with our emotions, and that we suffer. The *DSM*, as it defines its many disorders, presents a dispiriting picture of 'normalcy' (Kriss, 2013). The 'normal' individual is supposed to be mildly content all the time, but not too content, and apparently with no great passions in life. The normal person, and this includes young children, is able to behave in ways that others – bosses, teachers, etc. – find agreeable. The *DSM*, it could be argued, defines the 'good corporate' citizen, obedient to those in power, as 'normal.' Artists, rebels, and societal malcontents can all find themselves among the 'disordered.'

Moreover, in this modern therapeutic state, we are supposed to be on constant guard for signs that we are straying from this norm, and if so – if we are feeling anxious, depressed, or overly rambunctious – then we are prompted to conclude that something is wrong with us, and we need help. Equally harmful, we are told to see ourselves as under the control of mysterious chemicals in our brain. This encourages a sense of helplessness and promotes a sense that one is not responsible for one's self.

This brain disease model also serves as a barrier to social justice initiatives (and thus serves a neoliberal political agenda). Emotional and behavioral problems arise within the individual, and not in response to societal conditions. If the child is inattentive in school, it is the child's brain chemistry that is at fault, and not that the school may be failing the child. If a foster child is aggressive, or misbehaves, the child is said to have a psychiatric disorder and is medicated. The problem is located within the child; there is no societal need to provide a safe, nurturing environment for that child. And if adults who are struggling with poverty or working long hours at jobs that don't pay well find themselves stressed out and depressed, then the solution offered is an SSRI antidepressant. There is no need to look at income inequality, or societal structures, that can make life so difficult for so many.

### *Moving beyond the therapeutic state*

As can be seen in this brief history, there was a period, in the first decades of the nineteenth century, when treatment of the mad did not originate from within a medical context. The Quakers developed moral therapy in order to tend to 'brethren.' This is quite different from a therapeutic context, where doctors tend to patients. The Quakers professed to have no expertise in madness; they simply were providing a healing social environment. Moreover, researchers who have pored over asylum records have found that it was quite effective, producing recovery rates for seriously disturbed patients that have arguably never been matched since (Bockoven, 1972; Grob, 1973).

This brief historical review also makes it possible to see that the modern *DSM* era is the product of a medical guild's long rise and eventual triumph. In the early 1800s, physicians commandeered the Quaker asylums; the superintendents of the early asylums organized themselves into a guild; the guild subsequently presided over an expanding hospital culture; the guild then expanded into the community and started treating a much larger segment of the population; and finally, when its dominion over patients in the community was threatened, it relied on its societal status as a medical specialty to promote a story that, in essence, asserted its authority over all of American society. A medical guild with a history of feeling inferior to the rest of medicine, its members often derided as 'not real doctors,' successfully became the creators of a new society.

Moral therapy provides a model for moving beyond the therapeutic state today. Its success tells of how 'wellness' can be promoted by a nurturing social environment, as opposed to relying on professionals who can provide helpful treatment. The Quakers, by conceiving of the mad as 'brethren' (as opposed to patients), set forth a non-medical approach to helping those who are suffering in some way.

At the same time, once we understand how our modern therapeutic state came to be, and come to see it as a guild triumph, rather than as a narrative of scientific progress, then the public, angered at being duped, may be prompted to rebel, and seek to throw off this yoke of authority. Knowledge of this history can prompt a discussion, one populated by people from many walks of life and many countries, on how to strip psychiatry of its power. This, in my opinion, is the only way to free ourselves from a therapeutic state that is turning so many of us into patients: we must envision a future without psychiatry at the helm.

## References

American Psychiatric Association. (1980). *Diagnostic and statistical manual of mental disorders* (3rd ed.). Washington, DC: American Psychiatric Association.

American Psychiatric Association. (1994). *Diagnostic and statistical manual of mental disorders* (4th ed.). Washington, DC: American Psychiatric Association.

American Psychiatric Association. (2005, May 4). "Let's Talk About Depression," and "Mental illness stigmas are receding" [Press release].

American Psychiatric Association. (2013). *Diagnostic and statistical manual of mental disorders* (5th ed.). Washington, DC: American Psychiatric Association.

Andreasen, N. (1984). *The Broken Brain*. New York, NY: Harper & Row.

Bagalman, E., & Napili, A. (2015). Prevalence of mental illness in the United States: Data sources and estimates. *Congressional Research Service,* R43047, March 9, 2015.

Bockoven, J. (1972). *Moral treatment in community mental health*. New York, NY: Springer.

Buchanan, R. (2003). Legislative warriors: American psychiatrists, psychologists, and competing claims over psychotherapy in the 1950s. *Journal of the History of the Behavioral Sciences, 39*, 225–249.

Caplan, P. (1995). *They say you're crazy: How the world's most powerful psychiatrists decide who's normal*. New York, NY: Addison-Wesley.

Chase, A. (1980). *The legacy of Malthus*. Champaign, IL: University of Illinois Press.

Cullen, W. (1805). *Practice of physic*. New York, NY: L. Riley.

Dain, N. (1964). *Concepts of insanity in the United States, 1789–1865*. New Brunswick, NJ: Rutgers University Press.

Decker, H. (2013). *The making of DSM-III*. New York, NY: Oxford University Press.

Deutsch, A. (1937). *The mentally Ill in America*. New York, NY: Doubleday, Doran and Company.

Dix, D. (1843/1971). *On behalf of the insane poor: Selected reports*. New York, NY: Arno Press.

Frances, A. (2013). *Saving normal: An insider's revolt against out-of-psychiatric diagnosis, DSM-5, big pharma, and the medicalization of ordinary life*. New York, NY: William and Morrow.

Frontline, Public Broadcasting Service. (2001). *Medicating Kids, aired April 10, 2001. Supporting documentation: Federal laws pertaining to ADHD diagnosed children*. Retrieved from http://www.pbs.org/wgbh/pages/frontline/shows/medicating/schools/feds.html

Gorman, C. (1994, October 10). Prozac's worst enemy. *Time*, 64–65.

Greenberg, G. (2013). *The book of woe: The DSM and the unmaking of psychiatry*. New York, NY: Blue Rider Press.

Grob, G. (1973). *Mental institutions in America*. New York, NY: The Free Press.

Grob, G. (1983). *Mental illness and American society*. Princeton, NJ: Princeton University Press.

Grob, G. (1991). Origins of DSM-I: A study in appearance and reality. *The American Journal of Psychiatry, 148*, 421–431.

Grob, G. (1994). *The mad among us*. Cambridge, MA: Harvard University Press.

Hackett, T. (1977). The psychiatrist: In the mainstream, or on the banks of medicine. *The American Journal of Psychiatry, 134*, 432–434.

Harding, R. (2001, November 20). Unlocking the brain's secrets. *Family Circle*, 62.

Harris, G. (2011, March 6). DOCTORS, INC: Talk doesn't pay, so psychiatry turns instead to drug therapy. *New York Times*, A1.

Hillman, J., & Ventura, M. (1993). *We've had a hundred years of psychotherapy – And the world's getting worse*. New York, NY: Harper One.

Horwitz, A. (2002). *Creating mental illness*. Chicago, IL: The University of Chicago Press.

Horwitz, A., & Wakefield, J. (2007). *The loss of sadness*. Oxford: Oxford University Press.

Hunter, R. (1963). *Three hundred years of psychiatry*. Oxford: Oxford University Press.

Johnson, A. (1990). *Out of bedlam*. New York, NY: Basic Books.

Joint Commission on Mental Illness and Mental Health. (1961). *Action for mental health*. New York, NY: Science Editions.

Kevles, D. (1985). *In the name of eugenics*. Berkeley, CA: University of California Press.

Kriss, S. (2013, October 18). The book of lamentations. *TNI*.

Lacasse, J., & Leo, J. (2005). Serotonin and depression: A disconnect between the advertisements and the scientific literature. *PLos Med, 2*, 1211–1216.

Mayes, R. (2005). DSM-III and the revolution in the classification of mental illness. *Journal of the History of the Behavioral Sciences, 41*, 249–267.

Medco Health Solutions. (2011). America's state of mind Report, accessed at: http://apps.who.int/medicinedocs/documents/s19032en/s19032en.pdf.

Mehler, B. (1988). *A history of the American eugenics society, 1921–1940* (Ph.D. dissertation). University of Illinois at Urbana-Champaign.

Morton, T. (1895). *The history of the Pennsylvania hospital*. Philadelphia, PA: Times Printing House.

Myerson, A. (Ed.). (1936). *Eugenical sterilization: A reorientation of the problem*. New York, NY: Macmillan.

Robitscher, J. (Ed.). (1973). *Eugenic sterilization*. Springfield, IL: Charles C. Thomas.

Rogers, C. (1951). *Client-centered therapy*. Boston, MA: Houghton-Mifflin.

Rush, B. (1812/1962). *Medical inquiries and observations upon the diseases of the mind*. Reprint of 1812 edition. New York, NY: Hanger Publishing.

Scull, A. (1989). *Social order/mental disorder*. Berkeley, CA: University of California Press.

Shorter, E. (1997). *A history of psychiatry*. New York, NY: John Wiley & Sons.

Stotland, N. (2001, November 20). About depression in women. *Family Circle*, 65.

Strand, M. (2011). Where do classifications come from? The DSM-III, the transformation of American psychiatry, and the problem of origins in the sociology of knowledge. *Theory and Society, 40*, 273–313.

Tomes, N. (1994). *The art of asylum keeping*. Philadelphia, PA: University of Pennsylvania Press.

Tuke, S. (1813; reprinted in 1996). *Description of the retreat: An institution Near York, for insane persons of the society of friends*. London: Process Press.

Visser, S., Danielson, M., Bitsko, R., Holbook, J., Kogan, M., Ghandour, R., … Blumberg, S. (2014). Trends in the parent-report of health care provider-diagnosed and medicated attention-deficit hyperactivity disorders: United States, 2003–2011. *Journal of the American Academy of Child and Adolescent Psychiatry, 53*, 34–46.

Weiden, P. (1999). *Breakthroughs in antipsychotic medications*. New York, NY: W.W. Norton.

Whitaker, R. (2002). *Mad in America: Bad science, bad medicine and the enduring mistreatment of the mentally ill*. New York, NY: Perseus Press.

Whitaker, R., & Cosgrove, L. (2015). *Psychiatry under the influence: Institutional corruption, social injury, and prescriptions for reform*. New York, NY: Palgrave Macmillan.

Wilson, M. (1993). DSM-III and the transformation of American psychiatry. *The American Journal of Psychiatry, 150*, 399–410.

Zilboorg, G. (1941). *A history of medical psychology*. New York, NY: W.W. Norton.

# Children's mental health: Time to stop using psychiatric diagnosis

Sami Timimi

Hegemonic mental health service approaches stress the need for 'accurate' diagnosis in order to understand what the correct 'treatment' should be. I review the evidence on how far diagnosis in psychiatry has helped advance scientific knowledge and clinical practice and conclude that it hasn't. I then examine how National Institute for Health and Care Excellence (NICE) guidelines in relation to children's behaviour problems reflects the lack of progress that results from adopting a diagnostic approach. Taking mental health practice beyond reliance on narrow non-evidence-based diagnostic algorithms can be developed by adopting existing projects such as the Partners for Change Outcome Management Systems project.

Derzeit vorherrschende Ansätze für Dienstleistungen im Bereich der psychischen Gesundheit betonen die Notwendigkeit einer 'genauen' Diagnose, um zu verstehen, was die richtige Behandlung sein soll. Ich überprüfe zunächst, inwiefern Diagnosen innerhalb der Psychiatrie dazu beigetragen haben, den Stand der Wissenschaft und die klinische Praxis auch tatsächlich voran zu bringen – letztlich mit dem Schluss, dass dies nicht der Fall ist. Im Anschluss daran untersuche ich, wie sich dieser Sachverhalt in den Richtlinien des "National Institute for Health and Care Excellence" (NICE) in Bezug auf Verhaltensschwierigkeiten bei Kindern widerspiegelt. Dabei können die derzeitigen Methoden zur Behandlung von psychisch Kranken über den bisher gebräuchlichen Rückgriff auf einfache, nicht evidenzbasierte Algorithmen hinaus weiterentwickelt werden. Zum Beispiel indem bereits bestehende Projekte wie das "Partners for Change Outcome Management System" angewendet werden.

Los métodos hegemónicos de los servicios de salud mental, destacan la necesidad de establecer diagnósticos para saber cuál deber ser el "tratamiento correcto". Nos preguntamos si realmente el diagnóstico psiquiátrico ha contribuido al avance científico y a la práctica clínica y concluimos que no ha sido así. Examino cómo las directivas del Instituto Nacional de Excelencia Clínica (INEC), en relación con los problemas de conducta de los niños, reflejan la falta de progreso que resulta de adoptar el método fundamentado en diagnósticos. Llevar la práctica de la salud mental más allá de una estrecha dependencia basada en algoritmos diagnósticos de escasa evidencia, puede desarrollarse adaptando proyectos existentes como el de "Compañeros en Sistemas de Administración para Cambio de Resultados" (CSACR).

L'approccio egemonico presente nei servizi di salute mentale sottolinea la necessità di una diagnosi 'accurata' al fine di comprendere quale sia il 'trattamento' corretto. Riconsiderando le evidenze relative a come la diagnosi in psichiatria ha contribuito a far avanzare la conoscenza scientifica e la pratica clinica, si conclude che non ha rilevanza. Esaminerò quindi come le linee guida dell'Istituto Nazionale per la Salute e l'Eccellenza Clinica (NICE) in materia di problemi di comportamento dei bambini riflettano la mancanza di progressi che deriva da un approccio diagnostico. È possibile sviluppare la stima della pratica nell'ambito della salute mentale al di là del fare affidamento su algoritmi diagnostici non basati sulla stretta evidenza, utilizzando progetti esistenti, quali il progetto Partners for Change Outcome Management Systems.

Les approches hégémoniques des services de santé mentale insistent sur la nécessité d'un diagnostic 'précis' pour comprendre quel devrait être le 'traitement' adéquat. Dans cet article je cherche à savoir si le diagnostic en psychiatrie a contribué à l'avancée du savoir scientifique et de la pratique clinique et conclus que tel n'est pas le cas. J'examine ensuite comment les recommandations de l'Institut National pour la Santé et l'Excellence Clinique (NICE) concernant les problèmes comportementaux des enfants reflètent le manque de progrès résultant d'une approche basée sur le diagnostic. On peut développer une approche qui consisterait à porter la pratique de santé mentale au-delà du recours à des algorithmes diagnostiques qui ne sont pas fondés sur la preuve en adoptant des projets existants tels que le Partners for Change Outcome Management System.

Οι κυρίαρχες προσεγγίσεις των υπηρεσιών ψυχικής υγείας τονίζουν την ανάγκη για «ακριβή» διάγνωση, προκειμένου να κατανοήσουμε ποια θα πρέπει να είναι η σωστή «θεραπεία». Σε αυτό το άρθρο παρουσιάζω μια επισκόπηση των δεδομένων σχετικά με το κατά πόσο η ψυχιατρική διάγνωση έχει βοηθήσει στην εξέλιξη της επιστημονικής γνώσης και της κλινικής πρακτικής και καταλήγω στο συμπέρασμα ότι δεν έχει βοηθήσει. Στη συνέχεια εξετάζω πώς οι κατευθυντήριες γραμμές που παρέχει το Εθνικό Ινστιτούτο Υγείας και Κλινικής Αριστείας (NICE) σχετικά με τα προβλήματα συμπεριφοράς των παιδιών αντικατοπτρίζει την έλλειψη προόδου που προκύπτει από την υιοθέτηση μιας διαγνωστικής προσέγγισης. Προτείνεται ότι το να πάψουν οι πρακτικές της ψυχικής υγείας να βασίζονται σε μη τεκμηριωμένους εμπειρικά διαγνωστικούς αλγορίθμους μπορεί να αναπτυχθεί με την υιοθέτηση ορισμένων προγραμμάτων , όπως είναι το πρόγραμμα Partners for Change Outcome Management Systems.

Whilst the immaturity of children is a biological fact, the ways in which this immaturity is understood and made meaningful is a fact of culture (Prout & James, 1997). Members of any culture hold a working definition of childhood, its nature, limitations and duration based on a network of ideas that link children with other members of society and with the social ecology (Harkness & Super, 1996). In addition, different social practices of different cultures produce different childhoods each of which are 'real' within their local regime of truth (Stephens, 1995). People, 'know' themselves through the mediation of ideological institutions and some of the most important of these institutions, such as schools, focus their attention on children. Therefore, we cannot take at face value that individual actions evolve only from innate desires. Desires grow from norms, regulations and material circumstances interacting with the intentionality and agency of a person.

Such an ecological framework, that includes an appreciation of the intentional person making sense of their reality from within their broader social, political and cultural context, makes it difficult to pass a value or scientific judgement about whether children are better or worse off in any particular culture or society. In this way of thinking, the idea that there are universal ideals or natural unfolding process that all children should be able to achieve becomes suspect. This position also understands that children are socialised by belonging to a particular culture at a certain stage in that culture's history. This means that certain differences in children's behaviour can be seen as a result of different child rearing philosophies, socialisation processes and political realities.

## Rising rates of mental disorders in the young

Children, their behaviours and the meanings we construct about their behaviours, are a product of their socialisation and the socially constructed beliefs they, and others about them, have, as well as their biology. From this starting assumption, the treatment of childhood in current hegemonic psychiatric practice is troubling. Western psychiatry continues to argue that its concepts are universal 'truths' and that its diagnoses (such as ADHD, autism and childhood depression) are applicable and a way of making sense of childhood experiences across the globe. The outcome has been rapidly rising rates of diagnosis and prescriptions of psychotropic medication to children and adolescents.

Of particular concern is the increase in rate of stimulant prescription to children. In the US it is estimated that 11% of children aged between 4 and 17 have been diagnosed with ADHD and between half and two-thirds of these are then prescribed stimulants (Sharpe, 2014). In the UK prescribing of stimulants rose from about 6000 prescriptions a year in 1994 to over 1 million by 2013; a staggering 17,000% rise in two decades (NHS Information Centre & Health & Social Care Information Centre, 2015). These trends are being found with other psychotropic medications too (Timimi, 2009).

Have these rapid changes in practice in the area of children's mental health come about as a result of any major new scientific discovery? Below I outline the paucity of evidence supporting the use of a diagnostic approach to mental health problems in general and I highlight how such a context-poor approach can limit the way we respond to children.

## What did psychiatric diagnosis ever do for us?

Whilst prognosis for most conditions dealt with by the rest of medicine has improved, often reflecting genuine technical advances, no such progress has been seen in the prognosis of those who use mental health services.

The figures on outcomes from treatment in real-world mental health settings in the developed world are disappointing. Lambert (2010) concluded that 75% of people entering community mental health centres in the USA are either not responding to treatment, or deteriorating whilst in care. Hansen, Lambert, and Forman (2002), in a US study of over 6000 mental health service users, reported a picture of routine clinical care in which only 20% of clients improved. In Britain, The Centre for Social Justice (2012), reviewing the effectiveness data of a major project in National Health System mental health services, found only 15% of people entering the project were achieving 'recovery' by the time they left. In Australia, despite massive investment in mental health services in the past two decades, no corresponding improvement in the adult mental health of the population has been found (Jorm & Reavley, 2012).

A similar picture of poor outcomes in real-world Child and Adolescent Mental Health Services (CAMHS) has also been found. Weisz, Donenberg, and Weiss (1995) reported that for traditional treatment in the community, the overall effect size of change for those attending community child and adolescent health services compared to those who weren't, was close to zero, a finding replicated in further studies (Weiss, Catron, & Harris, 1999, 2000). Kazdin (2004) reported that 40–60% of youth who begin treatment drop out against advice. More recently, Warren, Nelson, and Burlingame (2009) and Warren, Nelson, Mondragon, Baldwin, & Burlingame (2010) found a deterioration rate of 24% amongst children in public community mental health settings.

Whitaker (2010) has documented a tripling of the number of disabled mentally ill in the US over the past two decades. In 1955, there were around 350,000 adults in the US state and county mental systems with a psychiatric diagnosis, but the number categorised as disabled from mental illness rose to 4 million adults by 2007. Similarly, the numbers of youth in America categorised as having a disability because of a mental condition leapt from around 16,000 in 1987 to 560,000 in 2007. Whitaker suggests these increases could be a direct consequence of a parallel increase in the use of psychotropic drugs, which may have long-lasting and negative impacts on a person's ability to function (Whitaker, 2010).

## Diagnostic approaches to mental health: the evidence

### *Aetiology*

The failure of decades of basic science research to reveal any specific biological or psychological marker that identifies a psychiatric diagnosis is well recognised. Unlike the rest of medicine, which has developed diagnostic systems that build on an aetiological and pathophysiological framework, psychiatric diagnostic manuals such as DSM 5 (American Psychiatric Association [APA], 2013) and ICD-10 (World Health Organisation [WHO], 1994) have failed to connect diagnostic categories with aetiological processes. Thus, there are no physical tests referred to in either manual that can be used to help establish a diagnosis. This lack of scientific progress connected to diagnostic groupings is a problem for research from a variety of perspectives, including biological research, where leading research groups are abandoning the use of current diagnostic systems (Insel, 2013; Owen, O'Donovan, Thapar, & Craddock, 2011).

Despite the belief that psychiatric disorders have a significant genetic loading, molecular genetic research is failing to uncover any specific genetic profile for any psychiatric disorder. Possible genetic abnormalities appear to account for only a small percentage of causal factors, and whatever genetic contribution has been found crosses diagnostic categories rather than having a distinct profile for each diagnostic category (Cross-Disorder Group of the Psychiatric Genomics Consortium, 2013).

The one notable exception to the lack of aetiological organisation in diagnostic systems is 'post-traumatic stress disorder' (PTSD), which implies that trauma leads to a particular and identifiable constellation of symptoms. However, there is a substantial body of evidence which finds that in the full spectrum of diagnoses in psychiatry, including psychosis, there is a greater likelihood of experiencing trauma and/or abuse (Bebbington et al., 2004; Varese et al., 2012).

### *Validity*

If we were to apply the standards found in the rest of medicine, then the validity of a diagnostic construct depends on the extent to which it represents a naturally occurring category. If it can 'carve nature at its joints', then there should be some identifiable properties beyond symptoms or behaviours, in those who have the diagnosis that can distinguish them from those who don't. The failure of basic science research to reveal any specific biological marker for psychiatric diagnoses means that current psychiatric diagnostic systems do not share the same scientific security, of belonging to a technological model developed by research grounded in the natural sciences, as the rest of medicine.

The frequency with which patients are given more than one diagnosis raises a concern about the specificity of diagnostic categories. Widespread co-morbidity (making more than one diagnosis in order to encompass patients' problems) indicates basic deficiencies in our understanding of the natural boundaries of even the most severe conditions that are diagnosed (Anckarsäter, 2010; Middleton, 2008). There is also a poor correspondence between levels of impairment and having the required number of symptoms for many psychiatric diagnoses. Thus, many below the threshold for a diagnosis have higher levels of impairment than those above, with many who reach the cut off for a diagnosis having relatively low levels of impairment (Kendler, 1999).

### *Reliability*

Reliability is the extent to which clinicians can agree on the same diagnoses when independently assessing a series of patients. Formal and operationalised diagnostic systems like DSM and ICD attempted to address reliability problems by imposing diagnostic agreement on the profession through the use of standardised diagnostic criteria via symptom checklists.

However, analysis of the studies involved in developing the first diagnostic manual that took this approach of 'operationalising' diagnosis through the checklist of symptoms approach (DSM-III, American and Psychiatric Association [APA], 1980) found that no diagnostic categories for which reliability was uniformly high. Ranges of reliability were found to be broad, and in some cases ranged the entire spectrum from chance to perfect agreement, with the case summary studies (in which clinicians are given detailed written case histories and asked to make diagnoses – an approach that most closely approximates what happens in clinical practice) producing the lowest reliability levels (Kirk & Kutchins, 1994). In DSM 5 field trials (Freedman et al., 2013), the kappa coefficients (a statistical measure of inter-rater agreement), were uniformly poor with some common diagnoses such as major depressive disorder and generalized anxiety disorder having levels of inter-rater agreement so poor, that what diagnosis you got was determined more by who you saw than what your problems was.

### *Treatment and outcome*

The technological paradigm that dominates is predicated on the assumption that the technical aspects of medical and psychological care are of primary importance and that making an 'accurate' diagnosis allows rational choice of the correct technical intervention.

However, the evidence finds that 'common factors', such as developing a strong therapeutic alliance, are much more important than therapeutic technique in determining outcomes (Bracken et al., 2012; Duncan, Miller, Wampold, & Hubble, 2009; Wampold, 2001).

Meta-analyses have concluded that the majority of variance in outcome as a result of therapy is accounted for by extra-therapeutic factors, whilst the quality of the therapeutic alliance accounts for most of the within-therapy variance in treatment outcome, and is up to seven times more influential in promoting change than treatment model used (Duncan, Miller, & Sparks, 2004; Wampold, 2001). This is also evident in 'real life' clinical encounters. For example, in a review of over 5000 cases treated in a variety of National Health Service settings in the UK, only a very small proportion of the variance in outcome could be attributed to psychotherapeutic technique, as opposed to non-specific factors such as the therapeutic relationship (Stiles, Barkham, & Mellor-Car, 2008).

The importance of non-specific factors is also found when using psychoactive drug treatments. The evidence supports the view that pharmacological agents are best conceptualised as inducing particular psychological states (rather than correcting chemical imbalances) that is not specifically related to diagnosis, but is nonetheless the basis for their usefulness (Moncrieff, 2009).

The lack of treatment specificity is not limited to the more common and less severe presentations. Thus patients outside the United States and Europe have much lower relapse rates, and are significantly more likely to have made a 'full' recovery and show lower degrees of impairment when followed up over several years, despite most having limited or no access to 'anti-psychotic' medication (Hopper, Harrison, Janka, & Sartorius, 2007).

Evidence is also accruing that, particularly in terms of functional outcomes, those who come off 'anti-psychotics' have better long-term outcomes than those who stay on them (Harrow, 2007; Wunderink, Nieboer, Wiersma, Sytema, & Nienhuis, 2013), adding further support to the importance of psychosocial approaches in treating psychosis. Klingberg and Wittorf (2012) in their review of evidence for psychosocial interventions for 'Severe Mental Illness', conclude that psychosis psychotherapy does not have an evidence problem but an implementation problem.

### *Colonialism*

For the last few decades, western mental-health institutions have been pushing the idea of 'mental-health literacy' on the rest of the world. A new global campaign for greater 'recognition' of mental illnesses in the non-industrialised world has developed, which assumes that ICD/DSM descriptions are universally applicable categories (World Health Organization, 2010). Cultures are viewed as becoming more 'literate' about mental illness the more they adopt western biomedical conceptions of diagnoses like depression and schizophrenia. In the process of doing this we not only imply that those cultures that are slow to take up these ideas are in some way 'backward', but we also export disease categories and ways of thinking about mental distress that were previously uncommon in many parts of the world. Thus, conditions like depression, PTSD and anorexia nervosa appear to be spreading across cultures, replacing indigenous ways of viewing and experiencing mental distress and opening up lucrative new markets for western drug companies (Summerfield, 2008; Watters, 2009).

Another impact on culture comes from psychiatric diagnoses inadvertently setting standards for 'normality', by categorising what emotional and behavioural traits and experiences should be considered 'disordered'. As the criteria for diagnoses are arrived at by subjective judgements rather than objective evidence (being literally voted in or out of existence by committees), they will likely have a bias towards the cultural standards found in economically dominant societies (who also tend to control what counts as 'knowledge' globally). This sets in motion a diagnostic system vulnerable to institutional racism in the dominant societies and colonialism in others, as other beliefs will, at least to some extent, come to be viewed as 'primitive', 'superstitious' etc., and their populations viewed as needing to be (psycho)educated (Timimi, 2012).

### *Cultural and public policy impact*

Diagnostic thinking has had a significant impact on service provision and public and professional beliefs about mental distress. It is widely argued that a large proportion of the population suffers from mental illness, that this amounts to a significant economic burden, and that there is a strong case for investing in improved mechanisms of detection and treatment for these disorders.

In order to increase rates of diagnosis and treatment, a variety of campaigns have been undertaken. For example, in the UK, the Royal College of Psychiatrists and Royal College of General Practitioners launched their 'Defeat Depression' campaign in the early 1990s (Paykel & Priest, 1992). Evaluations of this campaign found no evidence that it led to any significant improvements in clinical outcomes, but instead was associated with a rapid increase in antidepressant prescribing (Croudace, Evans, & Harrison, 2003).

Similarly research evaluating the 'Beyond Blue' campaign in Australia, which aims to increase awareness about depression and other mental disorders, demonstrated an increase in medical model beliefs about depression and an increase in rates of diagnosis of major depression between 1998 and 2008. It also noted a decrease in mental health related quality of life over this decade, and that having mental health literacy (i.e. a belief that depression was a medical diagnosis requiring medical treatment) that was categorised as 'poor' or 'fair', was a significant protective for recovery from major depression (Goldney, Eckert, Hawthorn, & Taylor, 2010) – in other words those who rejected the idea that their mental suffering was the result of a disease that needed medication, were more likely to recover.

The likelihood of positive outcomes for those with mental disorders is also further hampered by the stigma associated with the medical model (Sayce, 2000). Nearly all studies that have looked at public attitudes towards mental illness have found that the medical model for mental illness ('mental illness is an illness like any other illness') is associated with increased negative attitudes, greater fear of patients and a greater likelihood of wanting to avoid interacting with them (Angermeyer, Holzinger, Carta, & Schomerus, 2011).

### *Diagnosis-based approaches in mental health have hindered not helped*

For a diagnostic system to establish itself as scientifically useful, its categories should be able to 'carve nature at its joints'. For a diagnostic system to establish itself as clinically useful it should show that use of diagnostic labels aids treatment decisions in a way that impacts positively on outcomes. As reviewed above there is little evidence to support either position. There is much evidence to suggest that instead, they can cause significant harm. The only evidence-based conclusion therefore is that formal psychiatric diagnostic systems like ICD and DSM should no longer be used for either research or clinical practice.

## Children's behaviour problems: a NICE mess

An example of how diagnostic thinking causes confusion, contradiction and potential harms, can be found in the way in which clinical guidelines have been developed to reflect the narrow confines of diagnostic thinking. A brief review of three UK National Institute for Health and Care Excellence (NICE) guidelines related to children's behaviour illustrates this.

### *NICE guidelines on ADHD*

The NICE Quick Reference Guide on ADHD doesn't mention any concern or controversy over the concept of ADHD. The Full Guideline (which few will read) however has a more in-depth examination of validity (NICE, 2008). It is hard to understand how it was decided that ADHD met the standards they used to judge whether ADHD could be considered a 'valid' diagnosis.

For example, on the question of whether ADHD can be distinguished from normal variation they conclude 'Most analytic approaches are unable to make a clear distinction between the diagnosis of ADHD and the continuous distribution of ADHD symptoms in the general population' (NICE, 2008, p. 104). On genes they conclude 'As with all other types of risk factors associated with ADHD, the individual genetic variants associated with the disorder are neither sufficient nor necessary to cause it' (NICE, 2008, p. 111), and so on (for a more in-depth review of NICE ADHD guideline see Moncrieff and Timimi, (2012)).

NICE really departs from the evidence when it comes to finding support for using stimulant medication as a first line treatment. The review of pharmacotherapy studies notes the inadequate reporting of drug trial methodology, publication bias, limited reliability of results, inadequate data regarding adverse events and lack of evidence of long-term benefit, concluding that the evidence does not support using medication as a first line treatment for 'mild or moderate' ADHD. However, they also conclude that medication should be offered as a first line treatment in 'severe' ADHD with only one reference cited in support of this (Santosh, Taylor, Swanson, & Wigal, 2005), which concluded that in a 14-month randomised controlled trial, the more severe subgroup showed a larger decrease in symptoms from medication compared to behaviour therapy. Yet, a 36-month follow-up of the same patients, could not find support for continuing beneficial effects of medication over behaviour therapy, regardless of initial severity (Swanson et al., 2007). Other naturalistic studies have come to similar conclusions finding that medication offers little prospect of improving long-term outcomes (e.g. Currie, Stabile, & Jones, 2013).

### *NICE and autistic spectrum disorders*

NICE Autism guidelines encourage earlier recognition, which is likely to lead to a continuing increase in the numbers diagnosed with an autistic spectrum disorders (ASD) (Baird, Douglas, & Murphy, 2011). This guideline does not consider evidence on the validity of the diagnosis, assuming its validity is given. A diagnosis that is believed to be biologically driven and lifelong is at risk of causing significant harm through the negative impact of these assumptions on perceived competence, particularly if there are no objective findings to validate such a construct and no specific treatments available. The numbers are considerable as prevalence has expanded from 4 per 10,000 to 160 per 10,000 in just 4 decades – an over 3500% increase – but this impressive expansion has not come about through any new scientific discovery (Timimi, McCabe, & Gardner, 2010).

Although it is assumed that ASD must be genetic, thus far molecular genetic studies, including whole genome scans, have found evidence for a non-significant proportion of the assumed total genetic risk with these small genetic associations being heterogeneous, crossing psychiatric diagnostic boundaries and more strongly related to learning difficulties than a diagnosis of ASD per say (Hughes, 2012, p. S2). Similarly autism neuroimaging studies have been plagued by heterogeneity issues resulting in a characteristic lack of consistently replicated findings with new theories regularly arriving and then departing (Timimi et al., 2010).

There is also no evidence of methodologically sound and replicated research that demonstrates that particular interventions (whether educational, psychological, social or physical) specifically and differentially help those who have any form of autism (when compared to other children with behaviour or learning problems) (Timimi et al., 2010). With regard to prognosis, the same behaviourally defined syndrome (ASD) is applied to residents of institutions with little hope of living independently and has been suggested for men who have achieved greatness (such as Mozart, Van Gogh, Einstein, Edison, and Darwin). From an 'impairment' perspective, this is virtually the entire human spectrum, suggesting ASD, as it is defined, is too heterogeneous to have prognostic value. Not surprisingly prospective studies have shown remarkably diverse outcomes, with many who have been diagnosed with an ASD in childhood reportedly having little or no symptoms by adulthood (Szatmari, 2011).

### *NICE and conduct disorders*

Having painstakingly tried to avoid the possibility that ADHD or ASD could be thought of as being connected with adverse environmental experiences, when it comes to conduct disorders (CD) the reverse is true. CD we are told in the summary guide is associated with a greater likelihood of the child experiencing harsh and inconsistent parenting, parental mental health problems, environmental factors such as poverty and being looked after, and individual factors such as low educational attainment and other mental health problems. The treatment recommendations thus focus on parent training programmes and other systemic interventions (NICE, 2013).

### *Behaviour problems are not NICE compliant*

Rather than reflecting the considerable uncertainties inherent in the evidence concerning cause, treatment and outcomes, NICE (and I suspect our governments) would like us to believe that children presenting with behaviour problems can be accurately categorised and from there a correct (and one-dimensional) process for stopping deviant behaviour emerges. Sadly or gladly (depending on your perspective), in the real-world children's behaviour does not emerge out of predictable algorithms that enable us to accurately identify separate features caused by genes, parents, teachers etc., which then allows us to choose the 'correct' treatment. None of our medications treat a biological abnormality and none have been shown to improve long-term outcomes.

## An alternative approach: non-diagnostic practice

The main message from outcome research is that diagnosis driven models do not improve outcomes and services can improve outcomes by concentrating on developing meaningful relationships with service users that fully include them in decision-making processes (Bracken et al., 2012). Using flexible treatment models where there is regular testing through service user feedback of whether or not a particular intervention is improving outcomes for that service user has also been shown to improve outcomes and reduce the likelihood of becoming a 'long term' patient (Duncan, 2014).

One example of an approach that incorporates this evidence into a service delivery model is the Partners for Change Outcome Management Systems

(PCOMS) project. PCOMS is a project developed in the US that incorporates predictors of therapeutic success into an outcome management system that includes simple, easy to use ratings of both therapeutic progress and alliance (Duncan, 2014; Duncan et al., 2004). PCOMS has been shown in a number of randomised clinical trials to significantly improve effectiveness in clinical settings (Anker, Duncan, & Sparks, 2009; Reese, Norsworthy, & Rowlands, 2009; Reese, Toland, Slone, & Norsworthy, 2010). Several agencies have conducted systematic analyses of real-life implementations of PCOMS (see Bohanske & Franczak, 2010; Reese, Duncan, Bohanske, Owen, & Minami, 2014) finding that non-attendance and length of time in treatment decrease, while outcomes for service users are closer in magnitude to that found in research than in other studies of real-life services.

At the heart of the PCOMS approach is a non-diagnostic centred model of care incorporating systematic feedback of both outcome and alliance using non-symptom-based brief measures. Therapeutic sessions start with the outcome rating scale (ORS; Miller, Duncan, Brown, Sparks, & Claude, 2003). The ORS is a visual analogue scale consisting of four 10 cm lines, corresponding to four domains of functioning (individual, interpersonal, social and overall). Patients, and/or their supporters, place a mark (or click a mouse in the on-line versions) on each line to represent their perception of their functioning in each domain. Practitioners measure each line (this is done automatically in on-line versions) to get a score out of 10 for each domain and a maximum score out of 40 once all 4 scores are added up. Lower scores reflect more distress. Graphing session by session scores enables patients and practitioners to notice whether or not positive change is being perceived by the patient, enabling conversations about change to take place. If change isn't happening practitioners can discuss with patients, their supporters and colleagues, what might be done differently such as a change of therapeutic modality, change in who attends the sessions or indeed a change in practitioner.

The session rating scale (SRS; Duncan et al., 2003), also a four-item visual analogue scale, covers the traditional elements of the alliance, and is given towards the end of a therapeutic session. Using the SRS regularly, inserts a ritual into therapy. This prompts practitioners to have a conversation with their patients about their experience of therapy. The SRS provides a structure to keep the alliance at the forefront of the practitioner's thinking, allowing an opportunity to fix any problems, and demonstrating that the therapist does more than give lip service to the central task of forming good and empowering therapeutic relationships.

A UK-based implementation of the PCOMS approach – Outcome Orientated Approaches to Mental Health (OO-AMHS) (Timimi, Tetley, Burgoine, & Walker, 2013) – has also found similar positive outcomes following implementation in a CAMHS. Implementing OO-AMHS in a community CAMHS in Lincolnshire in the UK, moved practice away from a focus on diagnostic-based 'symptom management' paradigms and towards collaborative, patient and family empowering model of care, with treatments building on the primacy of relational aspects of care in preference to the primacy of technical ones. Evidence from implementation of the OO-AMHS approach within a community CAMHS in Lincolnshire found, after nearly two years of implementation, that the number of cases with the service for over two years had reduced from 38% of the caseload to 18%, numbers referred for in-patient treatment had also come down from 15 per year to 3 per year, and non-attendance rates had dropped significantly. Analysis of over 300 cases discharged from this team post implementation, found 77% of those discharged had shown clinically significant improvement and/or were above the clinical cut-off, with only 6% rating deterioration in their condition.

## Conclusion

Hegemonic mental health service approaches stress the need for 'accurate' diagnosis in order to understand what the correct 'treatment' should be. As reviewed above there is little evidence to support that such an approach leads to improved mental health services. There is much evidence to suggest that instead, it can cause significant harm.

For mental health services to progress, evidence on what does improve outcomes needs to be properly incorporated. Services that challenges hegemonic diagnostic models' oppressive stance towards empowering service users and recognising cultural diversity can be developed using existing templates such as that developed by the PCOMS project.

## References

American and Psychiatric Association. (1980). *Diagnostic statistical manual of mental disorders* (3rd ed.) (DSM-III). Washington, DC: Author.

American Psychiatric Association. (2013). *Diagnostic and statistical manual of mental disorders* (5th ed.) (DSM 5). Washington, DC: Author.

Anckarsäter, H. (2010). Beyond categorical diagnostics in psychiatry: Scientific and medicolegal implications. *International Journal of Law and Psychiatry, 33*, 59–65.

Angermeyer, M. C., Holzinger, A., Carta, M. G., & Schomerus, G. (2011). Biogenetic explanations and public acceptance of mental illness: Systematic review of population studies. *The British Journal of Psychiatry, 199*, 367–372.

Anker, M., Duncan, B., & Sparks, J. (2009). Using client feedback to improve couple therapy outcomes: A randomized clinical trial in a naturalistic setting. *Journal of Consulting and Clinical Psychology, 77*, 693–704.

Baird, G., Douglas, H. R., & Murphy, S. (2011). Recognising and diagnosing autism in children and young people: Summary of NICE guidance. *British Medical Journal, 343*, d6360.

Bebbington, P., Bhugra, D., Brugha, T., Singleton, N., Farrell, M., Jenkins, R., … Meltzer, H. (2004). Psychosis, victimisation and childhood disadvantage: Evidence from the second British National Survey of psychiatric morbidity. *The British Journal of Psychiatry, 185*, 220–226.

Bohanske, R. T., & Franczak, M. (2010). Transforming public behavioral health care: A case example of consumer-directed services, recovery, and the common factors. In B. L. Duncan, S. D. Miller, B. E. Wampold, & M. A. Hubble (Eds.), *The heart & soul of change: Delivering what works in therapy* (2nd ed., pp. 299–322). Washington, DC: American Psychological Association.

Bracken, P., Thomas, P., Timimi, S., Asen, E., Behr, G., Beuster, C., … Yeomans, D. (2012). Psychiatry beyond the current paradigm. *The British Journal of Psychiatry, 201*, 430–434.

Centre for Social Justice. (2012). *Completing the revolution: Commissioning effective talking therapies*. Retrieved from http://www.centreforsocialjustice.org.uk/client/media/Talking%20Therapies%20Paper.pdf

Cross-Disorder Group of the Psychiatric Genomics Consortium. (2013). Identification of risk loci with shared effects on five major psychiatric disorders: A genome-wide analysis. *The Lancet, 381*, 1371–1379.

Croudace, T., Evans, J., & Harrison, G. (2003). Impact of the ICD-10 Primary Health Care (PHC) diagnostic and management guidelines for mental disorders on detection and outcome in primary care: Cluster randomised controlled trial. *The British Journal of Psychiatry, 182*, 20–30.

Currie, J., Stabile, M., & Jones, L. E. (2013). *Do stimulant medications improve educational and behavioral outcomes for children with ADHD?* (NBER Working Paper No. 19105). Cambridge, MA: National Bureau of Economic Research.

Duncan, B., Miller, S., & Sparks, J. (2004). *The heroic client*. San Francisco, CA: Jossey-Bass.

Duncan, B., Miller, S., Sparks, J., Claud, D., Reynolds, L., & Brown, J. (2003). The session rating scale: Preliminary psychometric properties of a "working" alliance measure. *Journal of Brief Therapy, 3*, 3–12.

Duncan, B. L. (2014). *On becoming a better therapist: Evidence-based practice one client at a time* (2nd ed.). Washington, DC: American Psychological Association.

Duncan, B. L., Miller, S., Wampold, B., & Hubble, M. (Eds.). (2009). *The heart and soul of change: Delivering what works in therapy* (2nd ed.). New York, NY: American Psychological Association.

Freedman, R., Lewis, D. A., Michels, R., Pine, D. S., Schultz, S. K., Tamminga, C., … Yager, J. (2013). The initial field trials of DSM-5: New blooms and old thorns. *American Journal of Psychiatry, 170*, 1–5.

Goldney, R. D., Eckert, K. A., Hawthorn, G., & Taylor, A. W. (2010). Changes in the prevalence of major depression in an Australian community sample between 1998 and 2008. *Australian and New Zealand Journal of Psychiatry, 44*, 901–910.

Hansen, N., Lambert, M., & Forman, E. (2002). The psychotherapy dose-effect and its implications for treatment delivery services. *Clinical Psychology: Science and Practice, 9*, 329–343.

Harkness, S., & Super, C. (Eds.). (1996). *Parents' cultural belief systems: Their origins, expressions and consequences*. London: Guilford Press.

Harrow, M. (2007). Factors involved in outcome and recovery in schizophrenia patients not on antipsychotic medications. *Journal of Nervous and Mental Disease, 195*, 406–414.

Hopper, K., Harrison, G., Janka, A., & Sartorius, N. (Eds.). (2007). *Recovery from schizophrenia: An international perspective*. Oxford: Oxford University Press.

Hughes, V. (2012). Epidemiology: Complex disorder. *Nature, 491*, S2.

Insel, T. (2013). *Transforming diagnosis*. Retrieved from http://www.nimh.nih.gov/about/director/2013/transforming-diagnosis.shtml

Jorm, A. F., & Reavley, N. J. (2012). Changes in psychological distress in Australian adults between 1995 and 2011. *Australian & New Zealand Journal of Psychiatry, 46*, 352–356.

Kazdin, A. E. (2004). Psychotherapy for children and adolescents. In M. J. Lambert (Ed.), *Bergin and Garfield's handbook of psychotherapy and behavior change* (5th ed., pp. 543–589). New York, NY: Wiley.

Kendler, K. S. (1999). Setting boundaries for psychiatric disorders. *American Journal of Psychiatry, 156*, 1845–1848.

Kirk, S., & Kutchins, H. (1994). The myth of the reliability of DSM. *Journal of Mind and Behavior, 15*, 71–86.

Klingberg, S., & Wittorf, A. (2012). Evidence-based psychotherapy of schizophrenic psychoses. *Der Nervenarzt, 83*, 907–918.

Lambert, M. J. (2010). *Prevention of treatment failure: The use of measuring, monitoring, and feedback in clinical practice*. Washington, DC: American Psychological Association.

Middleton, H. (2008). Whither DSM and ICD, chapter V? *Mental Health Review Journal, 13*, 4–15.

Miller, S. D., Duncan, B. L., Brown, J., Sparks, J., & Claude, D. (2003). The outcome rating scale: A preliminary study of the reliability, validity, and feasibility of a brief visual analog measure. *Journal of Brief Therapy, 2*, 91–100.

Moncrieff, J. (2009). *The myth of the chemical cure*. Basingstoke: Palgrave Macmillan.

Moncrieff, J., & Timimi, S. (2012). The social and cultural construction of psychiatric knowledge: An analysis of NICE guidelines on depression and ADHD. *Anthropology and Medicine, 20*, 59–71.

National Institute for Health and Clinical Excellence. (2008). *Attention deficit hyperactivity disorder. Diagnosis and management of ADHD in children, young people and adults* (National Clinical Practice Guideline Number 72). London: Author.

National Institute for Health and Clinical Excellence. (2013). *Antisocial behaviour and conduct disorders in children and young people* (National Clinical Guideline Number 158). London: Author.

NHS Information Centre & Health and Social Care Information Centre. (2015). Retrieved from http://www.hscic.gov.uk/searchcatalogue

Owen, M., O'Donovan, M., Thapar, A., & Craddock, N. (2011). Neurodevelopmental hypothesis of schizophrenia. *The British Journal of Psychiatry, 198*, 173–175.

Paykel, E. S., & Priest, R. G. (1992). Recognition and management of depression in general practice: Consensus statement. *British Medical Journal, 305*, 1198–1202.

Prout, A., & James, A. (1997). A new paradigm for the sociology of childhood? Provenance, promise and problems. In A. James & A. Prout (Eds.), *Constructing and re-constructing childhood: Contemporary issues in the sociological study of childhood* (pp. 7–32). London: Falmer Press.

Reese, R., Norsworthy, L., & Rowlands, S. (2009). Does a continuous feedback model improve psychotherapy outcomes? *Psychotherapy: Theory, Research, Practice, Training, 46*, 418–431.

Reese, R., Toland, M., Slone, N., & Norsworthy, L. (2010). Effect of client feedback on couple psychotherapy outcomes. *Psychotherapy: Theory, Research, Practice, Training, 47*, 616–630.

Reese, R. J., Duncan, B., Bohanske, R., Owen, J., & Minami, T. (2014). Benchmarking outcomes in a public behavioral health setting: Feedback as a quality improvement strategy. *Journal of Consulting and Clinical Psychology, 82*, 731–742.

Santosh, P., Taylor, E., Swanson, J., & Wigal, T. (2005). Refining the diagnoses of inattention and overactivity syndromes: A reanalysis of the Multimodal Treatment study of attention deficit hyperactivity disorder (ADHD) based on ICD-10 criteria for hyperkinetic disorder. *Clinical Neuroscience Research, 5*, 307–314.

Sayce, L. (2000). *From psychiatric patient to citizen: Overcoming discrimination and social exclusion*. London: Macmillan.

Sharpe, K. (2014). Medication: The smart-pill oversell. *Nature, 506*, 146–148.

Stephens, S. (1995). Children and the politics of culture in "Late Capitalism". In S. Stephens (Ed.), *Children and the politics of culture* (pp. 3–53). Princeton, NJ: Princeton University, Press.

Stiles, W. B., Barkham, M., & Mellor-Car, J. (2008). Effectiveness of cognitive-behavioural, person-centred, and psychodynamic therapies in UK primary-care routine practice: Replication in a larger sample. *Psychological Medicine, 38*, 677–688.

Summerfield, D. (2008). How scientifically valid is the knowledge base of global mental health? *British Medical Journal, 336*, 992–994.

Swanson, J. M., Hinshaw, S. P., Arnold, L. E., Gibbons, R., Marcus, S., Hur, K., … Wigal, T. (2007). Secondary evaluations of MTA 36-month outcomes: Propensity score and growth mixture model analyses. *Journal of the American Academy of Child and Adolescent Psychiatry, 46*, 1003–1014.

Szatmari, P. (2011). New recommendations on autism spectrum disorder. *British Medical Journal, 342*, d2456.

Timimi, S. (2009). The use of psycho-pharmaceuticals to control boys' behaviour: A tale of badly behaving drug companies and doctors. *Arab Journal of Psychiatry, 20*, 147–160.

Timimi, S. (2012). Children's mental health in the era of globalisation: Neo-liberalism, commodification, McDonaldisation, and the new challenges they pose. In V. Olisah (Ed.), *Essential notes in psychiatry* (pp. 413–438). Rijeka: InTech.

Timimi, S., McCabe, B., & Gardner, N. (2010). *The myth of autism: Medicalising boys' and men's social and emotional competence*. Basingstoke: Palgrave Macmillan.

Timimi, S., Tetley, D., Burgoine, W., & Walker, G. (2013). Outcome Orientated Child and Adolescent Mental Health Services (OO-CAMHS): A whole service model. *Clinical Child Psychology and Psychiatry, 18*, 169–184.

Varese, F., Smeets, F., Drukker, M., Lieverse, R., Lataster, T., & Viechtbauer, W., … Bentall, R. (2012). Childhood adversities increase the risk of psychosis: A meta-analysis of patient-control, prospective- and cross-sectional cohort studies. *Schizophrenia Bulletin, 38*, 661–671.

Wampold, B. E. (2001). *The great psychotherapy debate: Models, methods, and findings*. Hillsdale, NJ: Lawrence Erlbaum.

Warren, J. S., Nelson, P. L., & Burlingame, G. M. (2009). Identifying youth at risk for treatment failure in outpatient community mental health services. *Journal of Child and Family Studies, 18*, 690–701.

Warren, J. S., Nelson, P. L., Mondragon, S. A., Baldwin, S. A., & Burlingame, G. M. (2010). Youth psychotherapy change trajectories and outcomes in usual care: Community mental health versus managed care settings. *Journal of Consulting and Clinical Psychology, 78*, 144–155.

Watters, E. (2009). *Crazy like us: The globalization of the American psyche*. New York, NY: Free Press.

Weiss, B., Catron, T., & Harris, V. (1999). The effectiveness of traditional child psychotherapy. *Journal of Consulting and Clinical Psychology, 67*, 82–94.

Weiss, B., Catron, T., & Harris, V. (2000). A 2-year follow-up of the effectiveness of traditional child psychotherapy. *Journal of Consulting and Clinical Psychology, 68*, 1094–1101.

Weisz, J. R., Donenberg, G. R., & Weiss, B. (1995). Bridging the gap between laboratory and clinic in child and adolescent psychotherapy. *Journal of Consulting and Clinical Psychology, 63*, 688–701.

Whitaker, R. (2010). *Anatomy of an epidemic*. New York, NY: Crown.

World Health Organisation. (1994). *International classification of diseases* (10th ed.) (ICD-10). Geneva: Author.

World Health Organisation. (2010). *mhGAP intervention guide*. Geneva: Author.

Wunderink, L., Nieboer, R., Wiersma, D., Sytema, S., & Nienhuis, F. (2013). Recovery in remitted first-episode psychosis at 7 years of follow-up of an early dose reduction/discontinuation or maintenance treatment strategy. *Journal of the American Medical Association: Psychiatry, 70*, 913–920.

# Psychiatric diagnoses, 'thought styles', and ex post facto fact fallacies

John Shotter

Living in two-way, *dialogical* relations with our surroundings, rather than in monological, one-way causal relations with them, means that we can no longer treat ourselves as inquiring simply into a world of objective 'things' already existing in the world around us. We need to see ourselves instead as always acting 'from within' a still-in-process world of flowing streams of intermingling activities affecting us as much, if not more, than we can affect them. In such a world as this, instead of discovering pre-existing things in our inquiries, we continually bring such 'things' into existence. So, although we may talk of having discovering certain nameable 'things' in our inquiries, the fact is, we can *only* see such 'things' as *having been at work* in people's activities *after* they have performed them. This, I want to argue, is also the case with all our diagnostic categories of mental distress – thus to see the 'things' they name as the *causes* of a person's distress is to commit an *ex post facto* fact fallacy. Something else altogether 'moves' people in the performance of their actions than the nameable 'things' we currently claim to have discovered in our inquiries.

Die Tatsache, dass wir in einer reziproken, dialogischen Beziehung mit unserer Umgebung stehen (und nicht in monologischen, einfachen Zusammenhängen), hat zur Folge, dass wir uns nicht länger als Akteure verstehen können, die einfach einer 'objektiv gegebenen Welt' gegenüberstehen und darin handeln. Vielmehr müssen wir unsere Handlungen als immanenten Teil einer sich ständig weiterentwickelnden Welt verstehen, als einen stetig ablaufenden Strom von sich kreuzenden Vorgängen, die uns und andere beeinflussen können. In einer solchen Welt treten wir 'vorgefertigten' Tatsachen nicht einfach gegenüber sondern sind an ihrer Entstehung stets beteiligt. Obwohl wir also manchmal davon sprechen, gewisse bedeutende Dinge durch Untersuchungen entdeckt zu haben, so kommen solche 'Dinge' doch nur vermittelt durch die und mit der Arbeit von Personen zum Vorschein. Dies, so mein Argument, ist auch der Fall bei unseren Diagnosekategorien für psychische Störungen - mit den 'Dingen', die sie als vermeintlich kausale Ursache einer psychischen Störung ausmachen, sitzen sie lediglich einer trügerischen weil nachträglichen Sinnzuschreibung auf. Dabei ist es, im Gegensatz zu benennbaren 'Dingen', etwas gänzlich anderes, was Personen in ihren Handlungen 'bewegt', und von denen wir doch gerade behaupten, dass wir sie in unseren Forschungen entdeckt haben.

Vivir en una relación dialógica (de dos vías) con nuestro ambiente, en lugar de una relación monológica (una sola vía) con él, significa que no podemos simplemente tomar una posición investigadora en el mundo de las ''cosas'' que ya existen a nuestro alrededor. Necesitamos vernos, al contrario, como actuando siempre' desde adentro'' de un proceso tranquilo en un mundo de corrientes fluidas de actividades entremezcladas, que nos afectan más de lo que nosotros las afectamos a ellas. En un mundo como tal, en lugar de descubrir con nuestras investigaciones cosas que ya existen, continuamente les damos existencia a tales cosas. De manera que cuando hablamos acerca de haber descubierto cosas ''nómbrales'', el hecho es que podemos ver solamente tales cosas como parte de las actividades de la gente después que ellos las han realizado. Quiero discutir que éste es también el caso con nuestra categorías de trastornos mentales, de manera que ver las cosas que ellos señalan como las causas de la aflicción de una persona, es cometer un acto de falacia ''ex – post – facto''. Algo más que las ''cosas'' nómbrales que nosotros aseguramos haber descubierto en nuestras investigaciones, es lo que mueve totalmente a la gente a llevar a cabo sus acciones.

Vivere in due modi, in relazioni dialogiche con i nostri contesti, piuttosto che in relazioni monologiche, con relazioni causali unidirezionali, a dire che non possiamo più considerare noi stessi come coloro che semplicemente indagano in un mondo di 'cose' già esistenti nell'ambiente che ci circonda. Abbiamo necessità di considerare noi stessi sempre come persone che agiscono 'da dentro' una realtà processuale, un mondo di attività mescolate che incidono su di noi tanto, se non di più, di quanto noi possiamo esercitare la nostra influenza. In un mondo come questo, invece di scoprire con le nostre indagini cose che preesistono, noi continuamente portiamo queste 'cose' entro l'esistenza. Così, sebbene si possa parlare di aver scoperto nelle nostre indagini particolari 'cose' denominabili, noi possiamo solo vedere queste "cose" come presenti nelle attività delle persone dopo che sono state eseguite. Quello che voglio discutere è anche il disagio mentale descritto con le categorie diagnostiche - così da vedere come le "cose" nominate quale causa del disagio di una persona è commettere un errore ex post facto. Qualcos'altro "muove" le persone nello svolgimento delle loro azioni rispetto alle 'cose' denominabili che attualmente sosteniamo di aver scoperto nelle nostre indagini.

Vivre de manière bidirectionnelle, en relation dialogique avec nos environnements, plutôt de de manière monologique dans une relation unidirectionnelle avec eux, veut dire que nous ne pouvons plus nous considérer comme investiguant un monde de 'choses' déjà existantes dans le monde autour de nous. Nous devons au contraire nous considérer comme toujours agissant 'au sein-même' d'un monde, toujours en devenir, fait de courants fluides d'activités s'entremêlant qui nous affectent autant, si ce n'est plus, que nous les affectons. Dans un tel monde, au lieu de découvrir des choses préexistant nos investigations, nous amenons continuellement 'les choses' à exister. Ainsi, bien que nous parlions d'avoir découvert grâce à nos investigations, certaines 'choses' nommables, le fait est que nous ne pouvons voir ces 'choses' qu'en tant qu'elles sont au travail au sein des activités des gens une fois accomplies. Je prétends que ceci est également le cas pour toutes nos catégories diagnostiques qualifiant la détresse psychologiques – ainsi voir les 'choses' qu'ils nomment causes de détresse d'une personne est en fait commettre une erreur de fait ex post facto. Contrairement à ce que nous déclarons avoir découvert grâce à nos investigations, quelque chose d'autre que les 'choses' nommables 'agit' les individus lorsqu'ils accomplissent leurs actions.

> Το γεγονός ότι ζούμε σε αμφίδρομες, διαλογικές σχέσεις με το περιβάλλον μας, παρά σε μονόδρομες αιτιακές σχέσεις με αυτό, σημαίνει ότι δεν μπορούμε πλέον να θεωρούμε ότι διερευνούμε απλώς έναν κόσμο με «αντικείμενα;/πράγματα» τα οποία προϋπάρχουν στον κόσμο γύρω μας. Αντίθετα, θα πρέπει να θεωρούμε ότι δρούμε «από μέσα» σε έναν κόσμο, ακόμη ασχημάτιστο, σε διεργασία, που αποτελείται από τη ροή αλληλένδετων δράσεων, που μας επηρεάζουν περισσότερο από ό,τι εμείς μπορούμε να τα επηρεάσουμε Σε έναν τέτοιο κόσμο, αντί να ανακαλύπτουμε προϋπάρχοντα πράγματα στις έρευνές μας, δημιουργούμε συνεχώς αυτά τα «πράγματα». Έτσι, αν και θα μπορούσαμε ίσως να πούμε ότι ανακαλύπτουμε και να κατονομάσουμε κάποια «πραγμάτα» στις έρευνες μας, στην πραγματικότητα μπορούμε να δούμε μόνο αυτά τα «πράγματα» ως μέρος της δράσης των ανθρώπων, μόνον αφού τα έχουν ήδη κάνει. Αυτό, θέλω να υποστηρίξω, ισχύει επίσης στην περίπτωση όλων των διαγνωστικών κατηγοριών που διαθέτουμε για τον ψυχικό πόνο- έτσι το να δούμε τα «πράγματα» που θεωρούμε ότι είναι αίτια του ψυχικού πόνου ενός ατόμου αποτελεί μια εκ των υστέρων (ex post facto fact) εσφαλμένη αντίληψη. Κάτι άλλο κινεί τους ανθρώπους να επιτελέσουν τις δράσεις τους από αυτά τα ονομασμένα «πράγματα» που σήμερα ισχυριζόμαστε ότι έχουμε ανακαλύψει στις έρευνες μας.

We need to remember that psychiatry, psychotherapy and psychological counselling are not physics, and that in *trying to care* for mentally distressed people, we are not (initially, at least) in the business of having to *prove* that our care *is in fact* 'care' – even if it later proves not to have been very effective care. We are not seeking to prove that our *verbalized predictions* are 'true' by showing that we can always, physically, 'make' them come true. We are not living within a physics-laboratory-world, but out in the complicated, multi-faceted and currently, very turbulent and disorderly world of everyday social activities, activities within which we are immersed, and which waft us this way and that, whether we like it or not. As living beings, we are creatures of our environment, our ecology. Indeed, as I write, in a letter to one of our national UK newspapers, 442 psychotherapists, counsellors and academics remark:

> The past five years have seen a radical shift in the kinds of issues generating distress in our clients: increasing inequality and outright poverty, families forced to move against their wishes, and, perhaps most important, benefits claimants (including disabled and ill people) and those seeking work being subjected to a quite new, intimidatory kind of disciplinary regime. (Guardian, 17th April, 2015)

Thus, as *primarily* carers, as practitioners, not research scientists, we are seeking *ways of being with* or *of relating to* other persons – *living, self-moving beings*, not a collection of separate particles in physical motion – who seem, so to speak, to have 'lost their way' forward in their lives, whose inner mental life is in such turmoil that they are unable to relate themselves to their surroundings in a 'healthy' way. Rather than seeking to understand what goes on inside their heads, our task is much more that of seeking to grasp what their heads go on inside of. Yet, a physics-laboratory approach to life still seems to be overwhelmingly influential. Competent professional reasoning is expected to be science-like. Why?

## Scientific thought

What, for some long time now we have 'taken as' *scientific thought*, emerged in the seventeenth century when developments in mathematics, physics, astronomy, biology (including human anatomy) and chemistry transformed our view as to what *proper thinking* about the 'external world' (Russell, 1914) should be like. Indeed, Descartes [1596–1650], in his *Discourse on the Method of Rightly Conducting the Reason, and Seeking Truth in the Sciences*, of 1637 set the scene for what we still seem to assume to be the actual nature of rational thought today: that it is a matter of abstracting a complex whole from its larger surroundings and breaking it down (analysing it) into its constituent parts in order to understand the causal relations between them, thus to manipulate them into a new, more desirable arrangement. Indeed, like many others at the time, he took our reasoning in geometry as a model for what our 'sure fire', unambiguous, reliable reasoning *should be like*; and he assumed it possible to think *about* everything in the same way: 'These long chains of reasoning, quite simple and easy, which geometers use to teach their most difficult demonstrations,' he said,

> had given me cause to imagine that everything which can be encompassed by man's knowledge is linked in the same way … [and consequently] there can be nothing so distant that one does not reach it eventually, or so hidden that one cannot discover it. (p. 41)

But what Descartes ignores here, as we will see, is our social lives, the shared background of *anticipations* that we come to embody as we first grow up into a particular linguistic (language-using) community, and come to selectively channelize in joining a professional group, along with the possibility that – as we have now come to realize – language does not work in the wholly *representational*, i.e. 'picturing' fashion that he imaged. Our wordings, our utterances, can have, as Wittgenstein (1953) points out, 'countless different kinds of use' (No. 23), other than merely, as nouns, standing for 'things', their *referents*.

## From 'atomic things' impacting on each other to our immersed 'movements' in flowing activities

Yet, from the beginning, as a major aspect of his way of thinking, the kind of world he thought of us as living in, was a world that could be *thought about* in terms of stable, spatial forms that could be represented in a one-to-one fashion by distinctive symbols. Sitting all alone in his warm, stove-heated room in

Germany, despairing of ever being able to refute the countless opinions voiced by all those around him, he 'resolved', he said,

> to speak only of what would happen in a new world, if God were to create, somewhere in imaginary space, enough matter to compose it, and if he were to agitate diversely and confusedly the different parts of this matter, so that he created a chaos as disordered as the poets could ever imagine, and afterwards did no more than to lend his usual preserving action to nature, and to let her act according to his established laws. (Descartes, 1968, p. 62)

A somewhat simplified view of physical reality that fitted in nicely with his also somewhat simplified view of how, what he called our *thinking*, takes place.

Descartes thus inaugurated a form of calculational, representational thought in which the 'reality' in which we had our being was 'pictured' as essentially mechanical and lifeless, but which we *animated*, so to speak, with our *thinking minds*. In other words, just as we might currently think of ourselves as *drivers* coming, habitually, to control of the *mechanisms of our cars*, so Descartes took it that as *minds* (as *res cogitans*) we are related to our *bodies* (as *res extensa*) in the same way: '... I am not only lodged in my body, like a pilot in his ship', he said, 'but, besides, that I am joined to it very closely and indeed so compounded and intermingled with my body, that I form, as it were, a single whole with it[1]' (p. 159). Thus, Descartes' world is a neutral 'container' for the working of our 'minds', an inert reality within which our minds work in terms of 'one-size-fits-all', lawful generalities that can, *ideally*, all play a role in a calculational form of reasoning.

Indeed, to go further, Descartes seems to take it that the thinking that we as adult thinkers *do deliberately* and know of ourselves as doing, as simply *what thinking is*. Whereas, in fact, it is drawn from, and is an aspect of, the thinking that *just happens within us* as a result of our having grown up within a particular language group, with its own particular cultural history, and of our later going on to operate as scientists within a particular, professional 'thought collective' with its own particular 'thought style' (Fleck, 1935/1979), along with its own particular *uses* of language (Wittgenstein, 1953). It is this kind of *just-happening*-'background'-*socially shared-thinking* that goes on within us – both, seemingly, out of our awareness and out of our own self-control – that 'sets the scene' for how we make sense of events occurring in our surroundings, and for the rest of what we do and say, both in relation to those events, and in relation to the others around us. Yet it is this not-easy-to-change, socially shared 'background', that we must change, if we are ever to conduct any truly *scientific* inquiries into our actual nature as living, social beings and not just elaborate either (1) notions of our own invention or simply (2) what is already familiar to us. We need to look into its genesis.

Thus in the alternative view I would like to introduce here, instead of living in a classical Cartesian world of separate particles in motion, I see us as living immersed within an oceanic world of ceaseless, intra-mingling currents of activity – many quite invisible – which in fact influence us much more than we can influence them. Rather than being like machines, with well-defined inputs leading to equally well-defined outputs, unresponsive to the larger contexts in which we must operate, we are thus much more like plants growing from seeds, rooted within many different intra-acting (Barad, 2007; Shotter, 2011), flowing streams of energy and materials that our bodies are continually working to *organize* in sustaining us as viable human beings. Buffeted by the wind and waves of the social weather around us, we inhabit indeterminate circumstances in which almost everything seems to merge into everything else; we do not and cannot observe this flow of activity *as if* from the outside. Thus, not only are we creatures of our environment, we are also continually uncertain as to *what* the situation *is* that faces us, and *how* we might act within it for the best within it. Indeed, as Merleau-Ponty (1962) makes clear: 'We must recognize the indeterminate as a positive phenomenon.' (p. 6). This, as we will see, gives rise to a very different view of psychological or mental distress than that enshrined in our current diagnostic categories.

## DSM, *ex post facto* fact fallacies and the difficulty of change

The DSM-5 was published on May 18, 2013. The response in Great Britain has not been favourable. It is 'Time for a Paradigm Shift in Psychiatric Diagnosis' suggested *The British Psychological Society's Division of Clinical Psychology* (DCP, 2013); 'The future of academic psychiatry may be social,' said Priebe, Burns, and Craig (2013) in *The British Journal of Psychiatry*. Yet, the likelihood of a radical change in our diagnostic practices is not great. Why?

I began this article as I did above, because in fact our thinking in the West is still infected with Cartesian ideas as to what proper, competent, professional forms of thought *should be like*. There is thus a major defect in how we conduct and report the nature of all our inquiries in our social and human sciences, not just in psychotherapy research – for our concern as rational professionals always to start our thinking, and to conduct our talking, in terms of *generalities* rather than *in relation to particularities*. In other words, to repeat, a particular 'thought style' (Fleck, 1935/1979) is at work in western intellectual culture at the moment, working always in terms, not simply in terms of *similarities* (and differences), but in terms of *samenesses* (A = A identities). And as Fleck makes clear: 'What actually thinks within a person is not the individual himself but his social community … . His mind is structured, and necessarily so, under the influence of this ever-present social environment and *he cannot think in any other way*' (p. 47); as a consequence: 'The explanation given to any relation can only survive and develop within a given society if this explanation is stylized in conformity with the prevailing thought style' (p. 2).

And further, along with the use of certain rhetorical devices – such as reference to 'scientific methods of investigation', 'objective evidence', 'random controlled trials', 'independent witnesses', etc. – those with competence in such procedures can construct their statements as 'factual statements', and claim authority for them as revealing a special 'true' reality behind appearances, without any reference to the everyday context of their claims. 'But this process can produce, and for us in the social sciences, *does* produce what Ossorio (1981) has called, *ex post facto* fact fallacies: the preclude retrospective claim that, for present events to be as they are, their causes *must* have been of a certain kind' (Shotter, 1993, p. 25). In attempting retrospectively to understand the origins and development of people's thought and actions, we describe their nature *now* within our to an extent finished and systematic schematisms. But this is totally ignore the fact for them, in their performance of them, they need to *feel forward*, so to speak, to sense the *fittingness* of their very step to their own *particular* needs and their own *unique* circumstances.

But the Cartesian *thought style* I outlined above, in still being at work in shaping our communication in our social and behavioural inquiries, precludes attention to particularities and uniqueness. Thus in our writings – with the aim of arriving at *generalities*, true for all time – after having described a circumstance in which a *particular* person *does* something, we often move (1) first from using the verb in question in the *active* to the *passive voice* – thus omitting the actual *human agent doing* the action – and (2) we then go on to *name* the activity in question as a 'thing' (albeit with agential powers). In short, our verbs become nouns. We then far too easily go on to treat the 'thing' in question – be it Social Anxiety Disorder; Intermittent Explosive Disorder; Bipolar Disorder; Bipolar Disorder; Attention-Deficit Hyperactivity Disorder; and so on – as a nebulous hidden agency at work in shaping our lives, without our being able to outline in any detail how such an influence *is* in fact at work in, or actually *came* to be so. As Billig (2013) remarks: 'What is strange is that social scientists accord higher status to grammatical forms that contain less information' (p. 120). For in the process, people as such are isolated from their surroundings, and turned into victims of hidden, *idealistic* forces seemingly *happening* to them out of their control, while their own efforts at *compensation* (see below) are ignored – bring in the experts!

This retrospective 'transformation' of (often still developing) activities with diffuse beginnings, occurring only in relation to particular people in particular contexts, into definite, self-contained 'things', thus eliminating people's own efforts at helping themselves, is pervasive in our thinking. It has, however, some very serious consequences in relation to our everyday practices; not least, is our tendency to look backwards *from* our identification of the 'thing' in question, *to* its supposed *causes within the individual concerned* – thus omitting the agency of the person in question, as well as their adjustive efforts in overcoming disturbances occurring to them in relation to events happening in their surroundings. We take the 'symptoms' expressed as indicative of the essentially hidden disorder.

## Symptoms as compensations – examples in opening up the 'not-yet-said' to intelligible expression

I want to begin this section with a psychotherapeutic incident that has intrigued me ever since I first read of it, an incident in which a 30 year old, revolving-door treatment failure – who had been hospitalized on several occasions for what had been diagnosed as paranoid schizophrenia – is talked to by Harry Goolishian (Anderson & Goolishan, 1992) who begins by asking Bill: 'What, if anything, could your previous therapists have done differently that would have been more useful to you?' And Bill replies:

> That is an interesting and complicated question. If a person like you had found a way to talk with me when I was first going crazy … at all the times of my delusion that I was a grand military figure … I knew that this [delusion] was a way that I was trying to tell myself that I could overcome my panic and fear … . Rather than talk with me about this, my doctors would always ask me what I call conditional questions … (p. 25)

What intrigues me about it, is that Bill clearly *senses* that he is *in* a very different relationship *with* Harry Goolishian, than with his other therapists, and he feels, immediately, able to speak of his 'delusions'. What was there 'in' Harry's *way of talking* with Bill – not in *what* he said, but in *how* he said it – that allowed Bill to make such an instant comparison between Harry and his other therapists, and furthermore, to go on to say:

> If a person like you had found a way to talk with me when I was first going crazy … then WE *could have handled that crazy general … I knew that this [delusion] was a way that I was trying to tell myself that I could overcome my panic and fear*?

What was 'there' in Harry's way of being with Bill that made it possible for Bill to express this?

The fact is, in our immediate *sensing* of the qualitative 'shape' of *how* the others around us are spontaneously *responding* to us, we can begin to anticipate how next they might act towards us, to anticipate how they will treat us as being *this* or *that* kind of person in the world.

Currently, psychiatric diagnoses are derived from observations of a patient's symptoms, as if the 'symptoms' we observe are direct indicators of a 'something wrong' with our inner workings. But are they?

Goldstein (1933/1995), a neurologist and psychiatrist studying brain damage from gun-shot wounds during the First World War, aware that what we might call *identity preserving* activities are always at work within living organisms when disturbed, voiced his worries about this method: 'We have become so accustomed to regard symptoms as direct expressions of the damage in a part of the nervous system,' he said,

> that we tend to assume that, corresponding to some given damage, definite symptoms must inevitably appear. We do so because we forget that normal as

> well as abnormal reactions ('symptoms') are only expressions of the organism's attempt to deal with certain demands of the environment. Consideration of this makes it evident that symptoms are by no means certain to become self-apparent. Symptoms are answers, given by the modified organism to definite demands: they are attempted solutions to problems derived on the one hand from the demands of the natural environment *and on the other from the special tasks imposed on the organism in the course of the examination.* (p. 35, my itals)

Indeed, a shift in a therapist's stance or attitude – from 'testing' to being 'exploratory', say – can be a major factor in influencing how clients/patients *feel* in relation to those around them, whether they feel that they will be responded to as a person of worth, or experience themselves as being seen as 'deficient' or as 'bad' in some way.

Thus, as *dialogical beings,* we do not and cannot put our thoughts and feelings into words simply as we please in our talk. We must 'fit' them appropriately into a context of other people's expectations. As Bakhtin (1986) puts it:

> An essential (constitutive) [aspect] of the utterance is its quality of being directed to someone, its *addressivity* … . the utterance has both an author … and an addressee … Both the composition and, particularly, the style of the utterance depend on … how the speaker (or writer) *senses and imagines* his addressees, and the force of their effect on the utterance. (p. 95)

Sensing and imagining what it is like to be a child, we shape our speech in one way (and talk slowly, clearly and with emphasis while addressing them), while talking to a speech recognition robot on the telephone, we shape it … well, perhaps in a similar manner … but if we talk to an adult friend 'like that', they would of course feel insulted … while how to talk to an expert stranger is a puzzle indeed.

Thus, as Goldstein (1933/1995) remarks goes on to say with respect to *aphasia*:

> … the difficulty in finding words, formerly regarded as the main symptom [of aphasia], retreated into the background. The theory of the reduced evocability of speech images became obsolete … since the patients are quite capable of using the words under specific circumstances … . The inability to find and use words voluntarily is not due to the primary defect of the speech mechanism but to *a change in their total personality which bars them from the situation in which meaning is required.* (pp. 37–38, my emphasis)

In other words, what Goldstein (1933/1995) emphasizes here is the need for a *comprehensive exploration* of the nature of a patient's/client's disturbance. Listening to a patient in such a way that *does justice* to *all* the details of their way of being in the world, would seem to be a crucial aspect of what it is for them to *feel* listened to.

Lampshire (2009), a voice-hearing service user, talks of needing sufficient time to tell her *complete* story in psychiatric interviews:

> … my wish is to share my thoughts and not to be analysed nor pathologized, but to be listened to. If you can listen to my complete tale and allow me to tell it without casting your own interpretation upon it, every clue and every nuance is there. Discerning the meaning behind my circumstances is a gift consciously and generously shared, and by having someone in your corner to share the burden, together we may free ourselves of the shackles'. (p. 184)

Debra Lampshire is unusual in having, to an extent, 'cured' herself of her 'nasty voices'. 'One of my earliest recollections,' she says,

> is an overwhelming feeling of not quite 'fitting in'; at school, within my family and within my environment. A sense of being on the outside looking in, of watching my life being lived as an observer, rather than a participant. Over time I was to have numerous experiences which would reinforce this sense of 'detachment' from others, and the more I experienced it the more I craved to experience the feeling of connection to others. (p. 178)

In other words, Lampshire experienced herself as *anxious* at having to live as *others* required her to live.

> If one wants to live the life *they choose* one has to be exposed to stress and learn how to deal with it. Essentially this is the art of growing up and dealing with an adult world in an adult way; I hadn't mastered this. I lived my live fuelled by childish notions and ill-conceived beliefs. (p. 182)

And in her own reflections on her bizarre behaviour, she now suggests that they have led her to the following premises:

- 'I was just simply being who I was, I didn't know how to be different.
- Others determined that I was without reason, I never ever felt that.
- I was living on instinct so deep and so profound it never occurred to me to question it' (p. 183).

And she continues by suggesting that the search

> for the cure is the greatest deception of all, for the search is an internal one. One of reconnecting to the self, discovering that you are entitled *to be*, and if you don't like that self, then it is your choice to change things. (p. 184)

We can find another similar example in Tanya Luhrmann's (2012) work. She talks of Susan, a big, imposing black woman who defends herself aggressively on the street, and who clearly meets the criteria for a diagnosis of schizophrenia – she thought that people listened to her through the heating pipes in her apartment, and heard them muttering mean remarks. But at the time Luhrmann met her, Susan was a success story; she had her own apartment, and was a student at the local community college. She had, however, resisted all attempts to diagnose her – even though that would have given her a right to housing – as the idea of 'being crazy' meant to her that she was too weak to handle life and that she had a broken brain that could never be mended. Susan had been the beneficiary of a new kind of intervention that simply gave people housing without them having to submit to a diagnosis. So although Susan knew that she had subsidized housing, she thought she had got it because she entered a programme to help her get off crack.

As Luhrmann (2012) remarks:

> Those who created programs like the one Susan is in believe that the social setting in which a patient lives and imagines herself have as much to do with her treatment as any medication … . People are more likely to accept housing when offered it in these programs than in care-as-usual settings, and after they are housed their symptoms lessen – whether or not they are taking medications. (p. 7)

My final examples come from Mukhopadyay (2000) and Higashida (2013), two severely autistic boys who, without having learned to speak, were taught to write by their mothers – Tito simply by his mother pointing the letters of the alphabet written on a piece of paper, and Naoki using a cardboard keyboard. Without going into too much detail, the point to make here is that both boys talk of not being in control of their own bodies: 'He felt that his body was scattered,' says Tito, 'and it was difficult to collect it together … . The helplessness of a scattered self was to taunt him for years together – even as I write this page' (p. 20). While Naoki writes: 'There are times when I can't act, even though I really, badly want to. This is when my body is beyond my control. I don't mean I'm ill or anything. It's as if my whole body, except for my soul, feels as if it belongs to someone else and I have zero control over it' (p. 68).

So again, the issue is to do with how others *respond to us* when we try to do things: 'It pains,' says Tito,

> when people avoid us [autistic people] and the schools refuse to take us. I faced it and felt that every day there may be others like me who are facing the social rejection like me. I must make the point clear that *it is not lack of social understanding which causes the weird behaviour, but it is lack of getting to use oneself in the socially acceptable way*, which causes the weird or the undesirable behaviour. (p. 57, my emphasis)

A lack of 'getting to use oneself' in the socially acceptable way. How could Tito possible learn such a skill if, from the start, everyone around him responded to him as weird, as not at all 'like us'? Naoki puts it this way:

> On our own we simply – don't know how to get things done the same way you do them. But, like everyone else, we want to do the best we possibly can. When we sense you've given up on us, it makes us feel miserable. So please keep helping us, through to the end. (p. 69)

Expressions of objection and anger are often misunderstood as disease symptoms, rather than as symptoms of bad communication. But for care there are consequences: mentally distressed persons react, not only to their own distress, but to how others react to them as a result of how they express their distress in relation to their surroundings.

## Conclusions

Thus, this 'after the fact' working backwards to a supposed *cause*, can easily give rise to so-called *ex post facto fact fallacies* – for example, the assumption, say, that *ADHD* (as a 'thing' at work within him or her) is the reason why a young person feels unable to focus on any one thing for any length of time. Whereas, the currently supposed neurobiological reason for the person's impulsive, disorderly behaviour – I don't want to deny the possibility of there being neurobiological reasons – may very well be found in the *particular* details of their upbringing within extremely disorderly social contexts, in their failure to have embodied many of our culturally developed ways of *relating ourselves* to events occurring in our surroundings, what elsewhere I have called 'ontological skills' (Shotter, 1984, 1989), *skills at being* a speaker, a listener, an observer, a person able to maintain a 'focus' on a topic of inquiry for a length of time and so on. However, such alternative accounts – couched as they will be in terms of *particularities* rather than *generalities* – cannot easily be offered, for they will fall on deaf ears.

Indeed, as Fleck (1935/1979) wrote:

> … once a statement is published it constitutes part of the social forces which form concepts and create habits of thought … [that come to determine] 'what cannot be thought of in any other way'… . There emerges a closed, harmonious system within which the logical origin of individual elements can no longer be traced. (p. 37)

These closed, harmonious systems of thought cannot be broken open by argument or by evidence from within – other, more 'moving', poetic ways are needed, along with the influence of user group 'outsiders', and the changed understandings of everyday folk. We fail to take the fact that, as living beings, people are just as much creatures of their environment as they are of their biology, sufficiently seriously. We need, once again, to open up our inquiries to the unique experiences of the unique persons of our concern.

## Disclosure statement

No potential conflict of interest was reported by the author.

## Note

1. It is evident here that Descartes is utterly unclear as to *what* he is in fact committing himself to in saying this. As I will argue later, *living wholes*, if we are to stay alive, we are indivisible wholes and cannot be "broken down", i.e. analysed, into a set of separate parts, as is required in his mechanistic philosophy, neither can we be thought of as existing in separation from our surroundings.

## References

Anderson, H., & Goolishan, H. (1992). The client is the expert: A not-knowing approach to therapy. In K. J. Gergen & S. McNamee (Eds.), *Therapy as social construction* (pp. 25–39). London: Sage.
Bakhtin, M. M. (1986). *Speech genres and other late essays*. (V. W. McGee, Trans.). Austin: University of Texas Press.
Barad, K. (2007). *Meeting the universe halfway: Quantum physics and the entanglement of matter and meaning*. Durham: Duke University Press.
Billig, M. (2013). *Learn to write badly: How to succeed in the social sciences*. Cambridge: Cambridge University Press.
DCP (2013). *Position Statement on Classification: Time for a Paradigm Shift in Psychiatric Diagnosis*. Retrieved from http://www.bpsshop.org.uk/Classification-of-behaviour-and-experience-in-relation-to-functional-psychiatric-diagnoses-Time-for-a-paradigm-shift-P3519.aspx, downloaded Feb, 2014.
Descartes, R. (1968). *Discourse on method and other writings*. (F. E. Sutcliffe, Trans. with introduction). Harmondsworth: Penguin Books.
Fleck, L. (1935/1979). *The genesis and development of a scientific fact*. Chicago, IL: Chicago University Press.
Gadamer, H.-G. (2000). *Truth and method* (2nd revised ed.). (J. Weinsheimer & D. G. Marshall, Trans.). New York, NY: Continum.
Goldstein, K. (1933/1995). *The organism: A holistic approach to biology derived from pathological data in man*. New York, NY: Zone Books.
Higashida, N. (2013). *The reason I jump*. London: Hodder & Stoughton.
Lampshire, D. (2009). Ramblings of an alleged mad woman. *Psychosis, 1*, 178–184.
Luhrmann, T.M. (2012). Schizophrenia. *Wilson Quarterly,* Summer, 28–34.
Merleau-Ponty, M. (1962). *Phenomenology of perception*. (C. Smith, Trans.). London: Routledge and Kegan Paul.
Mukhopadyay, T. R. (2000). *Beyond the silence*. London: National Autistic Society.
Ossorio, P. G. (1981). *Ex post facto: The source of intractable origin problems and their resolution* (LRI Report No. 28a). Boulder, CO: Linguistic Research Institute.
Priebe, S., Burns, T., & Craig, K. J. (2013). The future of academic psychiatry may be social. *The British Journal of Psychiatry, 202*, 319–320.
Russell, B. (1914). *Our knowledge of the external world*. London: Allen and Unwin.
Shotter, J. (1984). *Social accountability and selfhood*. Oxford: Blackwell.
Shotter, J. (1989). Social accountability and the social construction of 'you'. In J. Shotter & K. J. Gergen (Eds.), *Texts of identity* (pp. 133–150). London: Sage.
Shotter, J. (1993). *Conversational realities: The construction of life through language*. London: Sage.
Shotter, J. (2011). *Getting it: Withness thinking and the dialogical ... in practice*. Creskill, NJ: Hampton Press.
Wittgenstein, L. (1953). *Philosophical investigations*. Oxford: Blackwell.

# Radical presence: Alternatives to the therapeutic state

Sheila McNamee

This article introduces the idea of radical presence as an alternative to the current therapeutic state (or psy-complex) within which we live today. Radical presence challenges us to confront the dominance of psychological discourses which define, control, and limit the ways in which we live. It shifts our attention from diagnosis and treatment of individuals to an exploration of broader relational and institutional contexts, and the ways in which professionals and ordinary people alike can be responsive, present, and open to a multiplicity of life forms.

Der Artikel stellt das Konzept der radikalen Präsenz als Alternative zur gegenwärtigen Therapiegesellschaft (bzw. “Psy-Komplex“) vor. Radikale Präsenz hinterfragt die Dominanz des psychologischen Diskurses, welcher unser Leben bestimmt, beherrscht und begrenzt. Es ist der Versuch, unser Augenmerk weg von Diagnosen und Behandlungsformen, hin zu einer breiteren, relationalen und institutionellen Perspektive hin zu verschieben, und der damit verbundenen Möglichkeiten, damit Experten und ‘normale‘ Personen gleichermaßen responsiv, präsent und offen für eine Vielzahl von Lebensformen sein können.

Este artículo presenta la idea de la presencia radical como una alternativa para el presente estado terapéutico (o complejo ‘‘psi”) dentro del cual vivimos actualmente. La presencia radical nos desafía a confrontar la dominancia de los discursos psicológicos que definen el control y limitan la manera en que vivimos; desvía la atención del diagnóstico y tratamiento de los individuos hacia una exploración de contextos más amplios, relacionales e institucionales y las maneras en los cuales los profesionales y la gente común pueden ser receptivos y estar presentes y abiertos a una multiplicidad de formas de vida.

Questo articolo introduce l'idea della presenza radicale come alternativa allo stato terapeutico (o psico-complesso) entro cui viviamo oggi. Presenza radicale sfida a confrontarsi con i discorsi psicologici dominanti che definiscono, controllano e limitano il modo in cui viviamo. L'attenzione è spostata dalla diagnosi e dal trattamento degli individui ad una più ampia esplorazione di contesti relazionali e istituzionali e al modo in cui professionisti e persone comuni possono essere responsivi, partecipi e aperti a una molteplicità di forme di vita

Cet article introduit l'idée d'une présence radicale comme alternative à l'état thérapeutique actuel (ou complexe-psy) au sein duquel nous vivons aujourd'hui. La présence radicale nous met au défi de d'affronter la domination des discours psychologique qui définit, contrôle et limite nos vies. Elle déplace notre attention du modèle diagnostic/traitement des individus vers une exploration des contextes relationnels au sens large et vers les façons dont les professionnels comme les gens ordinaires peuvent être réceptifs, présents et ouverts à la diversité des formes de vie.

Αυτό το άρθρο εισαγάγει την ιδέα της ριζικής παρουσίας ως εναλλακτικής στην τρέχουσα θεραπευτική στάση (το λεγόμενο psy-complex), η οποία επικρατεί σήμερα. Η ριζική παρουσία απαιτεί από εμάς να αντιμετωπίσουμε την κυριαρχία των ψυχολογικών συστημάτων λόγου που καθορίζουν, ελέγχουν και περιορίζουν τους τρόπους με τους οποίους ζούμε. Μας προσκαλεί να μετατοπίσουμε την προσοχή μας από τη διάγνωση και τη θεραπεία ατόμων στη διερεύνηση των ευρύτερων σχεσιακών και θεσμικών πλαισίων και στους τρόπους με τους οποίους οι επαγγελματίες όπως και οι απλοί άνθρωποι μπορούν να είναι δεκτικοί, παρόντες, και ανοικτοί σε μια πολλαπλότητα των μορφών της ζωής.

## Introduction

A useful way to think about the therapeutic state is to reference Nikolas Rose's *Governing the soul: The shaping of the private self* (1990) and *Inventing ourselves: Psychology, power and personhood* (1998). In these now classic volumes, Rose draws upon Foucault's work (1965, 1972, 1973, 1977). Foucault and other post-structuralists argue that our sense of self, very much situated within the twentieth-century ideology of individuality, autonomy, free choice, and liberty, has been constructed by the rise in stature of the social and 'psy' disciplines. These disciplines (psychology, psychiatry, psychotherapy, psychoanalysis, sociology, and anthropology) have emerged as dominant discourses regulating our lives. Specifically, what a culture or society comes to believe is 'normal' is regulated by the psy-disciplines including normal sexuality, family life, and what we take to be rational.

To this extent then, we can say that we have been living in a 'therapeutic state' (Szasz, 1984) for the last century. It is a therapeutic state because, no matter what professional domain we encounter, we offer ourselves to the surveillance of experts – expert doctors, expert scholars, expert therapists, expert politicians, expert managers, etc. The move to reach beyond the therapeutic state is not a signal to obliterate psychotherapy or any of the psy-disciplines, nor is it to abolish any form of expertise. It is, rather, to envision alternatives to popularized, dominant, individualizing, and frequently pathologizing forms of life. It is to explore and imagine alternatives to individualized pathology. For some people, this may seem an odd endeavor, while for others it may even seem heretical. After all, there are people who have been diagnosed with psychoses, character 'deficiencies,' cognitive limitations, and behavioral digressions. The common belief is that these individual problems should be individually treated. But what if psychosis, character, cognitive, and behavioral oddities were not viewed as originating within an individual but were seen, instead, as expressions of diverse values and understandings – all emerging within different languaging communities? This article will explore this shift in focus as a move beyond the therapeutic state.

### *Pathologizing discourses*

Foucault makes clear that the disciplinary discourse referred to as the 'psy-complex' (Rose, 1990) is – just that – a discourse. It is a way of talking, a way of being in the world. And, to put it that way, suggests that there are or could be other ways of talking and being in the world available to us. This is not to suggest that psy-discourses are wrong or not useful. Rather, it is to suggest that, when engaged in the therapeutic encounter, we should ask ourselves how useful the concomitant vocabulary of psy-disciplines is – by this I mean the vocabulary of 'diagnosis,' 'pathology,' and 'mental disease.' This is most commonly located as an individualist discourse – one that places the nexus of a person's being within the private recesses of the mind/psyche (McNamee, 2002).

The concentrated focus on the individual in contemporary society is the byproduct of these emergent and eventually dominating discourses. And, when understood in historical, cultural, and social contexts, it becomes possible to recognize that all of us are active participants in the power and dominance of the psy-complex. As just one small illustration, most people unthinkingly seek professional therapeutic help when they encounter relational challenges or problems in their lives. In fact, what comes to be identified as a 'problem' or a 'challenge' is already inscribed by the naturalization of the psy-complex. If one is not perpetually happy and satisfied, there must be something wrong. If one member of a romantic couple seeks camaraderie outside the relationship, the union of the couple is in threat. If one is dissatisfied with one's work, there must be some problem with one's motivation. Basically, all problems we confront in contemporary society are traced to some personal failing or flaw within a modernist, individualist view. Furthermore, when an individual is 'working on' his or her problems with a professional, the common assumption is that the wisest action for those within the close network of relations is to stay away and let the professional do the work.

In just these simple illustrations, we see the deterioration of relational bonds. Where is the community to support one who is suffering? Who – if anyone – might be able to offer alternative descriptions of what one is experiencing, descriptions that are not pathologizing? Are work problems really due to an individual's lack of motivation, or might 'lack of motivation' be a rational response to an overbearing boss or competitive colleagues? A movement beyond the therapeutic state requires what I have come to call a 'radical presence' (McNamee, in press-a), that is, a multiplicity of resources for action. This fits, I think, with the necessary attentiveness to our embodied, daily interactions. An ethic of discursive potential provides us 'with the reflexive capacity to question common practices and to contest their 'truth status'. A relational ethic also embraces difference and complexity, eschewing the search for standardized practices' (McNamee, in press-b). Embracing a relational ethic requires that we abandon reliance on abstract principles and formal codes – not in an attempt to create chaos or anarchy, but in an attempt to *pay attention* to what is unfolding in the specific contexts and relations in which we find ourselves. Also, it is important to consider these local contexts *in relation to* the broader set of abstract ethical codes that have emerged into dominant discourses. This is not an ethic of 'anything goes'. Rather, it is an ethic of responsivity to self, others, and environment and, as such, demands that any local set of practices, beliefs, or values be considered in light of more dominant social practices. We might say that a move away from the psy-complex and its various discourses to a focus on interactive processes (communication) is a generative move beyond the therapeutic state. This opens space for how engaged participants can move beyond canonical understandings and forms of practice to co-construct generative and responsive alternatives.

To be clear, often the discourse of psychology and diagnosis can be very useful. And sometimes it can be dangerously damaging. If we simply use the tools of the trade (i.e. diagnosis) because 'that's what is supposed to happen' in psychotherapy, we are not radically present. We are not reflecting on how we collaborate in constructing the therapeutic process.

### Constructing a world

Elsewhere (McNamee, 2014), I have offered a visualization of the dialogic focus on interactive processes and how the responsiveness of persons to one another and to their environment comes to create what we 'know,' what we 'understand,' and what we believe to be 'real.' Let us consider how specific ways of understanding the world emerge. Meaning emerges as communities of people coordinate their activities with one another. These meanings, in turn, create a sense of moral order. The continual coordination required in any relationship or community eventually generates a sense of taken-for-granted, common practices otherwise known as dominant (and largely unquestioned) discourses.

As people coordinate their activities with others, patterns or rituals quickly emerge. These rituals generate a sense of standards and expectations that we use to assess our own and others' actions. Once these standardizing modes are in place, the generation of values and beliefs (a moral order) is initiated. Thus, from the very simple process of coordinating our activities with each other, we develop entire belief systems, moralities, and values. Of course, the starting point for analysis of any given moral order (reality) is not restricted to our relational coordinations. We can equally explore patterns of interaction or the sense of obligation (standards and expectations) that participants report in any given moment. We can also start with the emergent moral orders, themselves (dominant discourses as many would call them), and engage in a Foucauldian archeology of knowledge (1969) where we examine how certain beliefs, values, and practices originally emerged (which returns us to the simple coordinations of people and environments in specific historical, cultural, and local moments). The relational process of creating a worldview can be illustrated in Figure 1 as follows.

This is a simplified way of illustrating the relation among coordinated actions, emergent patterns, a sense of expectations, and the creation of dominant discourses. Adopting a radical presence focuses our attention on the specificities of any given interaction while also allowing us to note patterns across interactions, across time, place, and culture.

## *From mining the mental to radical presence: illustrations*

Thus far, my discussion of radical presence has been vague. My hope is that the notion is not conceptually vague or philosophically vague but I can imagine it, at this point, to be pragmatically vague. Yet, there is no technique, method, or specific strategy that accompanies radical presence. Instead, there is a way of positioning oneself in the world. Stewart and Zediker (2000), in their description of dialog (a form of interaction that I would claim requires and embodies radical presence), describe 'letting the other happen to you while holding your own ground' (p. 232). If you think about this, you recognize a dramatic shift from our ordinary, individualist way of operating in the world. Typically, we are taught to 'hold our own ground.' The persuasive rhetoric of everyday life requires us to hold our ground. Often the shift to a relational orientation such as the one I am presenting here is understood by critics as a position in favor of rampant relativism. If such were the case, holding one's ground would certainly not be championed with a relational stance. Yet, as we can see, the difference that makes a difference (as Gregory Bateson would say), is that one hold's one's own ground *while* being open to the other's orientation. Such a stance promotes neither debate-like forms of interaction nor interactions requiring complete surrender. My position (ground) is changed by virtue of considering yours. It is no longer me and my view against you and

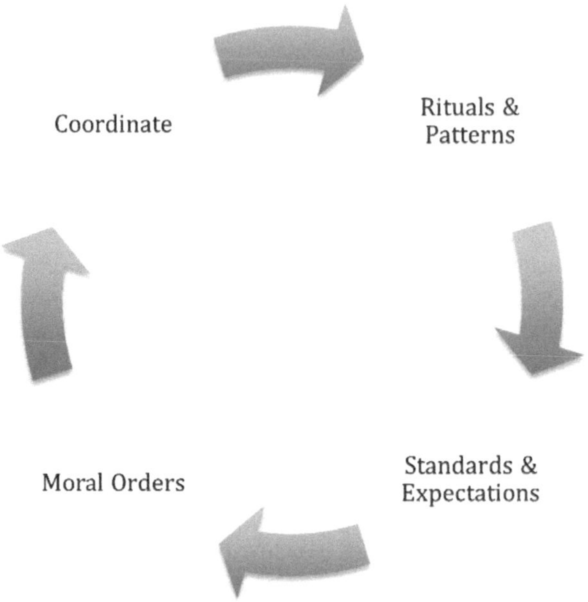


Figure 1. Constructing a World.

your view. It is my view in relation to your view. Dialog, as a form of radical presence, encourages curiosity for difference, openness to forming new understandings, and a movement away from agreement or adjudication of perspectives. Yet, the question remains: how can we put this into action? What follows are several illustrations of radical presence in action.

*Family care foundation*[1]

Carina Håkansson is the founder and leader of the Family Care Foundation in Sweden. She has written about the work of this foundation in her book, *Ordinary life therapy* (Håkansson, 2009). The foundation creates networks that can, in very ordinary ways, help seriously troubled individuals. Observing that the typical ways of treating people in distress (often people identified as psychotic) were not successful, Håkansson and her colleagues dared to imagine placing those who are troubled in ordinary family homes. She noted that hospitals, prisons, and institutions did little (or nothing) to assist a person in reclaiming his or her life. Yet, in building a community of support and respect by placing 'patients' in the homes of ordinary families, Håkansson and her colleagues have demonstrated the power of radical presence.

Håkansson (2009) does not claim that those who have been diagnosed as psychotic are 'normal.' What she claims is that everyone is 'normal' and 'abnormal' in different ways, in different contexts, and at different times. For example, a young man, confused about his future and feeling lost has a bad reaction to an argument with a friend, family member, or lover ... or perhaps he has what appears to be a psychotic episode after drinking or imbibing in some recreational drug. Any of these instances, if frozen in time, can warrant the label of psychosis and, if this is the case, the young man is most likely escorted to the local psychiatric institution. Once there, interviews (already couched within the medical frame of psychosis) seem to only prove the diagnosis. The more the young man resists, the more he becomes agitated, the more he perhaps becomes violent, the more 'accurate' the diagnosis. The consequential admission to the psychiatric hospital, complete with numbing doses of heavy medications follows. Each time the young man becomes once again agitated or 'difficult,' more medications are dispensed and more evidence is produced to insure that the diagnosis is correct.

How does one escape this cycle? It might not be exactly as described in the above scenario. The young man (or woman) might be taken to prison instead of a psychiatric hospital. In prison, the condemnation, the isolation, the fear, and humiliation provide ample support for the persistence of what becomes identified as criminal or psychotic behavior.

Breaking this pattern demands radical presence. It demands that instead of quick explanations provided by dominating understandings of what it means to be psychotic or criminal are (at least temporarily) put on pause. It means that what appears to be the obvious contextualization of the situation is questioned and that the context is broadened, the story expanded beyond the moment of digression, and alternative understandings are invited into the conversation.

When the Family Care Foundation places a person in a family home, that person is treated with respect. That person is treated as an 'ordinary' member of the household. This means that the newcomer is expected to pitch in, do the chores as other household members do. There is no attempt to figure out what is wrong with the 'stranger' but there is an attempt to integrate him or her into the flow of the family's life.

Here we see a beautiful illustration of radical presence. Both professionals and host families operate from the assumption that responsivity, respect, sensitivity to differences in dealings with issues of time and space can invite the 'psychotic' individual into an ordinary identity. It is an illustration of holding one's own ground while letting the other happen to you.

### *Isolation and addiction*

Johann Hari (2015) has written a compelling book about drug addiction. He travelled the world investigating this social problem. His work was heavily influenced by research conducted by psychologist Bruce Alexander in the 1970's (Alexander, 2008). Alexander (2008, in Hari, 2015) noted that both addiction to and withdrawal from drugs was not a chemical reaction as popularized in the media. At the time of Alexander's experiments, there was a popular antidrug advertisement on television. The advertisement portrayed a rat in a cage with a bottle of water laced with cocaine – identified as a deadly drug. The rat is shown returning over and over to the bottle to partake in more of the cocaine induced water. Eventually, the rat falls over dead. Alexander

(2008, in Hari, 2015), noted one feature of this advertisement that served to inspire his creative line of research: the rat was alone in the cage. He questioned the common wisdom about addiction based on his observations of and work with drug addicts. He proposed that drug addiction has less to do with the actual chemicals and the reaction of those chemicals on the brain. He proposed that addiction has more to do with environment and relations, and he

> … noticed something … rats had been put in an empty cage. They were all alone, with no toys, and no activities, and no friends. There was nothing for them to do but to take the drug. (Alexander, 2008, in Hari, 2015, p. 171)

Alexander (2008, in Hari, 2015) set out to explore the influence of environment on addiction. In his study, there were two rat cages. One that contained an isolated rat with two bottles: one with water and one with morphine. In the second cage, the cage Alexander called the 'Rat Park,' he provided wheels, balls, good food, and instead of putting one rat in the cage alone, he put several rats in together. The second cage, like the first, had two bottles: one with water and one with morphine. What Alexander observed was that the rats in the Rat Park drank 'less than 5 milligrams' of the morphine while the rats in the isolated cages 'used up to 25 milligrams of morphine a day' (Alexander, 2008, in Hari, 2015, p. 172). Even more interesting was that

> He took a set of rats and made them drink the morphine solution for fifty-seven days, in their cage, alone. If drugs can hijack your brain, that will definitely do it. Then he put these junkies into Rat Park. Would they carry on using compulsively, even when their environment improved? … In Rat Park, the junkie rats seemed to have some twitches of withdrawal – but quite quickly, they sopped drinking the morphine. A happy social environment, it seemed, freed them of their addiction. (Alexander, 2008, in Hari, 2015, p. 172)

There's much more to be said about this and the interested reader is encouraged to read Hari's book (2015). But the question for us is, what does this have to do with radical presence and alternatives to the therapeutic state? Everything. In Hari's description of Alexander's research, we see strong support for a social, relational approach to human problems. It is an approach that diverges from the 'go to' method of individual diagnosis and treatment. Paying attention to a person's relational environment – not just with other humans but the physical environment as well – offers a wealth of resources for transforming problems. When we expand beyond the individualized, medicalized approach, we recognize that those suffering have options. Perhaps, the options are choices made between participating in certain relationships over others. Or perhaps alternative forms of explanation can be generated once we expand our attention beyond the singular person. This too, is what radical presence is about. It requires a curiosity, a responsivity, and a desire to understand beyond what appears to be 'obvious.' Alexander (2008, in Hari, 2015) illustrated just such radical presence in noticing – the very simple act of noticing – one small but significant factor: isolation vs. relational engagement.

*Community outreach*

As another illustration of radical presence in action, Holzman (2015a) reports some very interesting results of a community survey focused on lay opinions of diagnosis and medication. She reports that for the past few years she and her colleagues have spent time on the streets of New York City surveying ordinary people about biologically based diagnosis. They wanted to know what would be 'effective ways to involve people in learning about alternatives and, for those who wanted more choices, in shaping new approaches in collaboration … with like-minded professionals' (Holzman, 2015b). The results of the survey indicate that

> Everyone offered an alternative [to diagnosis and medication], with most people suggesting more than one. The most frequent responses involved talking to people – therapy, counseling, group therapy being the most common (including, 'A center they can go to without getting diagnosed'), followed by family, friends, self-help and support groups.
>
> A wide variety of social activities and life style changes were recommended – volunteering, hobbies, music, dance, writing, meditation, exercise, yoga, diet, prayer and creating community … (Holzman, 2015b)

What the respondents in Holzman's report are suggesting is that, when faced with problems, *interaction with others* is often more useful than diagnosis. In fact, as Hari (2015) illustrates in the case of addiction, problems that are currently described as 'chemical,' 'biological,' or 'neurological' are often the byproduct of social relations. This raises an important question: Are we obliged to inquire into an alternative understanding of personal suffering? What would happen if our attention was diverted from searching for the proper diagnosis, evaluation, assessment or answer, and instead focused on examining broader social conditions and how 'problems' might actually be logical responses to these conditions? This is the focus that will direct us beyond the therapeutic state. Like Håkansson (2009), Hari (2015), and Alexander (2008), the community outreach spearheaded by Holzman (2015a, 2015b) and her colleagues is rooted in radical presence.

## Radical presence as a different path for going on together

To me, it is clear that radical presence positions us to appreciate a relational understanding of the social world. With so many traditions, beliefs, and values to coordinate, how could unanimity be possible, how could some abstracted form of understanding/knowledge be possible? The world is complex, not simple. It is time that we embrace this complexity and develop ways of *coordinating complexity* rather than eliminating it by providing 'expert diagnoses' to decontextualized or partially contextualized actions. That is what brings us to a radical presence in the daily, mundane interchanges of life. After all, wouldn't it be more generative to replace the impulse to resort to the normalized practices constructed by dominant discourses with the impulse to be curious about differences? Let's not define coordination of difference as agreement; let's define it as understanding (where understanding does not mean agreement, evaluation, or judgment – it simply means generating curiosity about difference). Our respectful attempts to understand might foster new forms of coordinated activity and this coordination might be focused on tolerance of difference – a radical presence.

If we focus our attention on *how* the perpetuation of undesirable situations is not the sole problem of a specific individual but is the byproduct of particular forms of life – that is, ways of living in community – we might begin to see both how to transform those patterns into novel ways of going on together in the world and how to appreciate difference as a natural part of social life – not necessarily something that must be repressed, avoided, or minimized. We need to widen the lens; we need to see and assess what is happening within our communities, our institutions, and our culture. Important questions to ask include: How does therapy for my problems assist me in generating strong relational bonds? How do diagnosis, evaluation, and assessment help me appreciate the relations that show support and care? Can we harness the potential of coordinating differences to move beyond simple solutions and universal resolutions? What if we began to view difference as a resource for creativity, novelty, and social transformation?

As long as we shelter ourselves within the discourse of psychology, we avoid confronting some of the most vexing challenges of today. When problems are individual problems, we can treat, punish, or educate individuals to 'fit in' to the preferred view of social life. If instead we ask ourselves how our broader social structures and our ways of maintaining those social structures contribute to alienation, disengagement, humiliation, degradation, and negative evaluation, we recognize our own participation in the perpetuation of individualized pathology. By adopting a radical presence, we can move beyond the therapeutic state and harness the vast resources available when multiple communities coordinate together to create ways of 'going on together' (Wittgenstein, 1953).

## Note

1. To learn more about the Family Care Foundation, go to http://www.familjevardsstiftelsen.se/

## References

Alexander, B. (2008). *The globalization of addiction: A study in poverty of the spirit.* Oxford: Oxford University Press.

Foucault, M. (1965). *Madness and civilization.* (R. Howard, Trans.). New York, NY: Random House.

Foucault, M. (1972). *Archeology of knowledge.* (A. M. Sheridan Smith, Trans.). New York, NY: Pantheon.

Foucault, M. (1973). *The birth of the clinic.* (A. M. Sheridan Smith, Trans.). New York, NY: Pantheon.

Foucault, M. (1977). *Discipline and punish.* (A. Sheridan, Trans.). New York, NY: Pantheon.

Håkansson, C. (2009). *Ordinary life therapy.* Chagrin Falls, OH: Taos Institute Publications.

Hari, J. (2015). *Chasing the scream: The first and last days of the war on drugs.* New York, NY: Bloomsbury.

Holzman, L. (2015a). Survey on emotional distress and mental health diagnosis: An international campaign to include "regular people" in the conversation. Retrieved from Mad in America: http://www.madinamerica.com/2015/07/survey-on-emotional-distress-and-mental-health-diagnosis-an-international-campaign-to-include-regular-people-in-the-conversation/.

Holzman, L. (2015b). A report on community outreach: Lay opinions on emotional distress and diagnosis. Retrieved from DxSummit.org: http://dxsummit.org/archives/2249.

McNamee, S. (2002). The social construction of disorders: From pathology to potential. In J. D. Raskin & S. K. Bridges (Eds.), *Studies in meaning: Exploring constructivist psychology* (pp. 143–168). New York, NY: Pace University Press.

McNamee, S. (2014). Research as relational practice: Exploring modes of inquiry. In G. Simon & A. Chard (Eds.), *Systemic inquiry: Innovations in reflexive practice research* (pp. 74–94). London: Everything is Connected Press.

McNamee, S. (in press-a). The ethics of relational process: John Shotter's radical presence. In T. Corcoran & J. Cromby (Eds.), *Joint action: Essays in honor of John Shotter.* London: Routledge.

McNamee, S. (in press-b). Ethics as discursive potential. *The Australian and New Zealand Journal Of Family Therapy.*

Rose, N. (1990). *Governing the soul: The shaping of the private self.* New York, NY: Routledge.

Rose, N. (1998). *Inventing ourselves: Psychology, power and personhood.* Cambridge: Cambridge University Press.

Stewart, J., & Zediker, K. (2000). Dialogue as tensional, ethical practice. *Southern Communication Journal, 65*, 224–242.

Szasz, T. (1984). *The therapeutic state: Psychiatry in the mirror of current events.* New York, NY: Prometheus Books.

Wittgenstein, L. (1953). *Philosophical investigations.* Oxford: Blackwell.

# The extended therapy room

Carina Håkansson

Family Care Foundation was created in 1987 as a reaction towards a system which far too often seems to forget it is real people involved, both those called clients and professional helpers. It is as if knowledge from ordinary life often is put aside when entering a professional context. Manuals and specific methods have increased steadily over the years as also psychiatric diagnosis and prescription of pharmaceuticals. It is argued here that regardless of whether we are called therapists, family homes or clients, we are affected by each other and the situations we find ourselves in. We bear with us our personal history while we are also part of a larger context. Those of us working as psychotherapists have a potential to contribute with knowledge regarding human beings and human life conditions. This paper describes and discusses some central themes found in practice and through research. In psychotherapy, as in life, there are moments and situations that can't be proven or verbally explained, which perhaps can't be completely understood. Our shared work in the Extended Therapy Room entails, as in life, moments of deepest fear as well as moments of wonderful joy.

Die "Family Care Foundation" wurde damals im Jahr 1987 als Reaktion auf ein System gegründet, welches allzu nur oft vergessen hatte, dass in ihm reale Menschen, Klienten und Professionelle agieren. Es scheint so, als würde in einem professionellen Kontext oftmals das Alltagswissen beiseitegeschafft. In den letzten Jahren haben zudem Handbücher und spezifische Techniken ebenso wie psychiatrische Diagnosen und Verordnungen konstant zugenommen. Hier wird die Ansicht vertreten, dass, unabhängig davon, ob wir Therapeuten, ein Familienheim oder Klienten sind, wir uns gegenseitig und von den Situationen Beeinflussen lassen in der wir uns befinden. Wir führen unsere je eigene persönliche Geschichte mit während wir gleichzeitig Teil eines größeren Ganzen sind. Jene von uns, die als Psychotherapeuten arbeiten, besitzen mit ihrem Wissen die Möglichkeit, einen positiven Beitrag für die Menschen und deren Lebensbedingungen zu leisten. Der vorliegende Artikel beschreibt und diskutiert einige zentrale Themenstellungen aus der Praxis und Forschung. In der Psychotherapie, wie im Leben generell, gibt es Momente und Situationen, die weder überprüft noch kommunizierbar sind und zum Teil auch gar nicht vollständig verstanden werden. Unsere gemeinsame Arbeit im erweiterten Therapieraum bringt, wie allgemein im Leben, Momente tiefster Angst als auch wundervoller Freude mit sich.

La Fundación para el Cuidado de la Familia fue creada en 1987 como una reacción hacia un sistema que demasiado frecuentemente parece olvidar que se involucra a personas reales, ambos, los llamados clientes y los profesionales que les prestan ayuda. Es como si el conocimiento acerca de la vida ordinaria se dejase de lado cuando se entra en el contexto profesional. Desde hace varios años ha aumentado el número de manuales y métodos específicos de tratamiento, así como también los diagnósticos psiquiátricos y la prescripción de fármacos. En este artículo se discute que, sin tomar en cuenta si somos terapeutas, hogares familiares o clientes, cada uno de nosotros afecta al otro y viceversa, así como nos afectan las situaciones en las cuales nos encontramos. Llevamos con nosotros nuestra historia personal mientras que al mismo tiempo somos parte de un contexto mayor. Los que trabajamos como psicoterapeutas tenemos un potencial para contribuir con conocimientos en relación con el ser humano y las condiciones humanas de vida. Este artículo describe y discute algunos temas centrales encontrados en la práctica diaria y en la investigación. En psicoterapia como en la vida, hay momentos y situaciones que no pueden ser comprobadas o explicadas verbalmente y que quizás no puedan ser totalmente comprendidas. Nuestro trabajo compartido en el "Consultorio Extendido" conlleva como en la vida misma, momentos del más profundo miedo, así como momentos de maravilloso disfrute.

La Family Care Foundation è stata creata nel 1987 come reazione ad un sistema che troppo spesso sembra dimenticare che sono coinvolte persone reali, sia quelle chiamate clienti sia i professionisti dell'aiuto. Quando ci si colloca entro un contesto professionale, si rischia di mettere da parte la conoscenza della vita quotidiana. Manuali e metodologie specifiche sono andate aumentando costantemente nel corso degli anni, così come la diagnosi psichiatrica e la prescrizione di farmaci. In questo contributo si sostiene che, a prescindere dal fatto che siamo chiamati terapeuti, case famiglia o clienti siamo tutti colpiti dalle vicende e dalle situazioni in cui ci troviamo. Portiamo con noi la nostra storia personale, e contemporaneamente siamo parte di un contesto più ampio ancorché coloro che lavorano come psicoterapeuti abbiano un potenziale di conoscenza per aiutare gli esseri umani e favorire condizioni di vita umane. Questo articolo descrive e discute alcuni temi centrali della pratica clinica e della ricerca. In psicoterapia, come nella vita, ci sono momenti e situazioni che non possono essere mostrati o verbalmente spiegati, e che forse non possono essere completamente compresi. Il nostro lavoro nella stanza di Terapia Estesa comporta, come nella vita, momenti di profonda paura, così come momenti di gioia meravigliosa.

La Family Care Foundation a été créée en 1987 en réaction contre un système qui trop souvent semble oublier que ce sont de vrais gens qui sont impliqués, que ce soient ceux qu'on appelle les clients ou les aidants professionnels. C'est comme si le savoir émanant de la vie ordinaire était souvent écarté lorsqu'on entre dans un contexte professionnel. Au cours des années, manuels et méthodes spécifiques n'ont cessé de proliférer tout comme les diagnostics psychiatriques et les prescriptions pharmaceutiques. Cet article avance que quelle que soit notre appellation - thérapeutes, clients, maison familiale – nous nous affectons les uns les autres et sommes affectés par les situations dans lesquelles nous nous trouvons. Nous portons en nous notre histoire personnelle tout en faisant partie d'un plus large contexte. Ceux d'entre nous travaillant comme psychothérapeutes peuvent potentiellement apporter leur contribution grâce à leur savoir concernant les êtres humains et leurs conditions de vie. Cet article décrit et discute certains des thèmes centraux que l'on trouve dans la pratique et dans la recherche. En psychothérapie, comme dans la vie, il y a des moments et des situations qui ne peuvent être prouvés ou expliqués verbalement, ce qui ne peut pas complètement être compris peut-être. Notre travail commun dans la salle de consultation élargie comprend, comme dans la vie, des moments de peurs profondes mais aussi des moments de joies intenses.

Το Family Care Foundation ιδρύθηκε το 1987 ως μια αντίδραση απέναντι σε ένα σύστημα το οποίο πολύ συχνά φαίνεται να ξεχνά τους εμπλεκόμενους σε αυτό πραγματικούς ανθρώπους - τόσο τους αποκαλούμενους πελάτες όσο και τους λεγόμενους επαγγελματίες . Μοιάζει σαν η γνώση από την καθημερινή ζωή συχνά παραμερίζεται όταν μπαίνει κανείς σε κάποιο επαγγελματικό πλαίσιο. Τα εγχειρίδια και η διατύπωση συγκεκριμένων μεθόδων έχουν αυξηθεί σταθερά με την πάροδο των ετών, όπως επίσης και η ψυχιατρική διάγνωση και συνταγογράφηση των φαρμάκων. Υποστηρίζεται εδώ ότι, ανεξάρτητα από το αν αποκαλούμαστε θεραπευτές, οικογενειακά ιδρύματα ή πελάτες, επηρεαζόμαστε ο ένας από τον άλλο και από τις καταστάσεις στις οποίες βρισκόμαστε. Κουβαλάμε μαζί την προσωπική μας ιστορία, ενώ είμαστε επίσης μέρος ενός ευρύτερου πλαισίου. Όσοι από εμάς εργάζονται ως ψυχοθεραπευτές έχουμε τη δυνατότητα να συνεισφέρουν με τις γνώσεις μας σχετικά με τα ανθρώπινα όντα και τις συνθήκες ζωής τους. Το παρόν άρθρο περιγράφει και αναλύει μερικά κεντρικά θέματα που προέκυψαν από την κλινική πράξη και μέσω της έρευνας. Στην ψυχοθεραπεία, όπως και στη ζωή, υπάρχουν στιγμές και καταστάσεις που δεν μπορούν να αποδειχθούν ή να εξηγηθούν λεκτικά, και ίσως να μην μπορούν να κτανοηθούν πλήρως. Το κοινό μας έργο στο Δωμάτιο της Διευρυμένης Θεραπείας εμπεριέχει, όπως και στη ζωή, στιγμές βαθύτατου φόβου, καθώς και στιγμές μεγάλης χαράς.

## To start with practice

For more than 25 years, I have been involved in a project with a diverse group of people; we come from many different backgrounds and we speak different languages, in the sense that we use our own words and express ourselves in different ways. These project members include therapists, clients, and those offering family homes.

To give you a sense of how this might work in practice, I will start with a story. This is one of 14 stories included in my doctoral thesis, which attempted to explore what is most important in my experience as a psychotherapist in the Extended Therapy Room (Håkansson, 2014).

> We're sitting on a veranda with a view over fields and woods. A number of dogs, big and small, are twirling around my feet. One of them is particularly insistent on getting my attention and wants to sit on my lap. Just as I pick the dog up I glance at the boy sitting across from me. He doesn't have a dog in his lap, which makes instantly question whether or not I should have one in mine.
>
> We've been here once before, this boy and I. That time I had a colleague with me and she is here with us again today. This is good because she knows the family home well and they have been through a lot together. They have worked together for more than five years and my colleague has been their supervisor twice.

How do I describe the meeting I and the others are in the middle of? How to explain in writing what isn't expressed in words, just something you feel in your body? Looks exchanged, sighs let out, hearts that beat a little fast.

I'll make a stab at it since I have become more and more convinced that this is actually what therapy is, at least a kind of therapy. A therapy that can't be captured in a manual, can't be reported by ticking the boxes in a formula. This is a different kind of therapy.

The boy has been 'a problem' for years. That was how he defined himself the first time we met. He defined himself as a monster, a problem child, an ADHD kid that was impossible.

The boy has lived in several different places during his relatively short life. Early on in life, he was diagnosed with a number of psychiatric disorders and prescribed the heavy medication associated with them. He has lived through, like so many of the people I meet in my work, more than anyone should ever have to experience. This has affected him in various ways. He has a hard time trusting and he doesn't always know what he himself or others actually mean by what they say and do. Sometimes he has a terrible temper! He has a wonderful sense of humor, a great fantasy, and an eye for things that aren't always easy to see. He is smart and notices almost everything, including how well what was said and then what was done tally.

The family home consists of two parents and their two adult children who live on the farm in their own separate houses. They usually eat dinner all together, but the rest of the time they all live their own lives. They help each other when one of them needs help. Sometimes they fight, but usually they all get along and they like each other a lot. This is the impression I get when I'm sitting with them on the veranda and our conversation slowly develops.

I say something on the order of that even though this has been my job for almost 25 years, I still think that it's both wonderful and remarkable when new people meet and begin to get to know each other. My colleague nods and says she feels the same way. We're silent for a moment. The mother in the family offers us a cookie and I register that the boy takes one, and then another. This is a good sign.

Then my colleague says that when we come next time, if the boy is still there of course, we'll bring crab because he likes them. 'That would be great,' the father in the family says 'because we've never eaten crab. We don't know how.' The boy grins but doesn't say anything. The mother says they often buy shellfish when they are in town, but never crab. 'It seems kind of hard to eat.'

Once again it gets quiet. I notice that the boy now has a dog in his lap. I think that I'd like to pick mushrooms in the woods when we drive back into town. I haven't done that for a long time.

I don't remember who started but we begin to talk about painting and drawing. The father in the family home tells us that the mother once painted a whole wall like a fairytale in their former house. The son's eyes shine when he remembers what the kitchen wall look liked. His mother had illustrated his and his sister's favorite fairytale on that wall.

'I'm dyslectic,' the father says and explains that he had to make up his own stories when his kids were little. He describes how he would sit with them under each arm while he told his story. 'Sometimes you fell asleep and the kids were so disappointed,' his wife says. He smiles but doesn't say anything. I think this just might turn out alright. This just might be the place where the boy can be himself, together with these people and with my colleague and I on the side but still with them.

In many ways, this is a completely improbable constellation, the boy and this family home. And yet it isn't. They have some things in common, like a love of animals and artistic creativity. That can make for a good beginning. We'll have to find a way to solve the rest as we go along, and we all need to realize this is going to demand a lot from all of us.

What do I mean when I say this is going to require a lot from us? I mean we have to be prepared to handle anxiety and uncertainty, cussing and the feeling of insufficiency. We have to trust each other, but we also have to trust ourselves. What we have ahead of us won't fix itself. We'll have to put our hearts and souls into it and each one of us will have to struggle to find the best way we each can contribute.

We will have our structure to lean on; the regular team meetings, supervision for the family home, conversations between me and the boy, usually with one of the family parents participating part of the time, and then the big meetings when anyone who can be of help is welcome to join.

Although the structure is a good support all our years of experience, all the stories that have taken form over the years and other important persons' thoughts and experience are keys in each of our lives. Things like books, films, plays, the subtle reflections that life every now and then proffers.

For my part, add all the years in the village where I grew up, my close family and big, motley extended family, counts and alcoholics, dogs and horses, old people and kids. They all play a part in the glorious mishmash of a life that wasn't anything else than that. It was only later in life that I learned to categorize and theorize, for better or worse, in a way I still can't quite explain. (Håkansson, 2014, p. 36)

## The Family Care Foundation

The Family Care Foundation was created in 1987 through a shared vision to attempt to maintain a good place where 'clients' would be given the chance to make sense of their life situation, in order to understand something essential about their lives and their history.

From the outset, the idea was to make use of ordinary life knowledge in a professional therapeutic context. 'Clients' would live in a family home, which is a kind of foster home, and at the same time maintain therapeutic conversations. The family home would receive supervision and support to handle the new situation in which one of our clients lived in their home and shared their lives.

When the project started, we were two young social workers, without any therapeutic training, who had conversations with both the family home and the client, sometimes together and sometimes separately. In one constellation, the professional helper might be a supervisor for the family home, and in another they would be the client's therapist. The idea behind this was that we would learn both how to handle individual conversations, and to find the best way to guide family homes without getting 'too attached' to our ideas about our own work or 'what a client or family home was like.'

Over time, both our work and the therapeutic room have been extended and now comprise considerably more people and contexts. I now meet people who wonder how it was at all possible and my answer to that is that we had to trust the family homes, our clients, their families, and ourselves.

As years have passed, I have come to realize the importance of our early lack of academic and therapeutic training. If it had not been for that lack, we would probably not have been so eager to learn from each other in daily practice. We had to listen to each other, and to try to understand what was happening in the very moment.

## Family home

A family home is a kind of foster home that invites someone or, in some cases, several persons (a parent with children) for a period of time to share their life with them. We try to find families that are willing to 'open their homes and hearts,' not just for the person who lives with them, but for that person's family and the therapists that are part of the team. It is crucial to have a desire to participate in the shared commitment and have an open relationship with those who live in their home and the therapists involved in the work.

Many family homes are located in the countryside and a few are in cities. Almost all the family homes have children of different ages, but we also work with family homes without any children. Some of the family homes' children are adults with families of their own.

We look for family homes with a different identity from that of being a 'professional helper.' The majority live in close proximity to both animals and nature and almost everyone thinks daily contact with animals is very important, a necessity actually. There is a certain value in living close to nature and having animals around, but we don't always require it as we also work with family homes which are close to big towns. This is because some of our clients cannot or do not want to live in the countryside. It's important that the family home is well-rooted in the place where they live since this opens up opportunities for clients to be invited into the local society, and it facilitates their finding a place for themselves there.

## Clients

The people I refer to as clients are all ages. We work together with adults, teenagers, and parents that come with their children. The common denominator is that people coming to our organization have experiences of crisis in already-difficult lives. Almost all of our clients have been in contact with social services and/or psychiatric services for some years, and four out of five have at least one psychiatric diagnosis when contacting us. Many people describe how they have lost hope that life is possible to live. Some have taken drugs for a long time. Others have major relationship problems. People often describe their life situation as very difficult and they are longing for something else than what social services and psychiatry represent.

We also meet children, teenagers, and adults who don't stay in one of our family homes, but who come to us for psychotherapy due to our experience and knowledge about the importance of relationships in a context without psychiatric diagnoses, and with support to reduce or withdraw from pharmaceutical drugs.

## Abolishing psychiatric diagnosis and concepts

Family Care Foundation started as a reaction towards a system which far too often seems to forget there are real people involved, both 'clients' and 'professional helpers.' Far too often, it is as if essential knowledge from ordinary life is put aside when entering a professional context, as if things like time, trust, and authentic relationships are no longer valid.

Being part of an ordinary context has affected the way my colleagues and I talk both talk about and talk to the people we meet. A person in someone's home need neither be defined as a client nor as a patient with a psychiatric diagnosis. The person staying in one of our family homes is a human being in all their complexity and diversity. In someone's home, you are and you do what people in common are and do, and the words used to depict this are so-called ordinary words. You are tired, angry, sad, upset, and perhaps even crazy at times. In someone's home, you are a human being among other human beings, a person in a situation together with others who in different ways influence and are influenced by each other, as always when people come together.

Many years ago, when we decided not to use psychiatric diagnoses in our practice, we could not know how it would affect our future. Nonetheless, we took the decision because it was no longer possible to do anything else. Our decision was influenced by our many years of shared work with family homes. Language in daily life is different from specific psychological and psychiatric terminology. In someone's home, people speak to each other in a different way than on a psychiatric ward.

Another reason not to use diagnoses is the uncertainty surrounding the construction of current classifications. There is a great deal of ambiguity, and at times outright error, concerning the assumption of connections between a person's situation in life, their behavior, and their symptoms. Far too many times, we had met people who had been given a diagnosis without them or their families understanding what it meant and we witnessed the harm it caused.

### Extending the therapeutic framework

Family Care Foundation started from a shared vision to try and create a place for people who, for a while in their lives, needed other people around them (Håkansson, 2009). This was fundamental and the professional framework was secondary. In other words, it was less important to decide exactly how long a conversation could take or where it would take place. We didn't find it important to maintain a certain order in a conversation or follow a specific method or theory. We had a different mission. We wanted to make space for allowing the creation of meaning to emerge between people.

By extending the therapeutic framework, it becomes possible to see and hear more, or to express this in another way; to see and hear *something else.* An example of this is the interruptions that occur, primarily in the family home, both in daily life as well as in the therapeutic conversations that are held in the family home. These interruptions, or framework breaches in a traditional therapeutic sense, have broadened our perspective on psychotherapy and what is possible and not possible to do in a therapeutic context. The interruptions also clarify the question of what is important in the therapeutic conversation and context.

Early on in my career, I felt joy and meaning when working together within a family home because being in that context so clearly included me both as a social worker and as the person 'Carina.' But also because I never knew what was going to happen next. All of a sudden we might be interrupted, something that disturbed and was unexpected. For example, a vet might arrive when we were talking about something emotionally painful with the person living in the family home. Despite this, we would have to interrupt our conversation because the vet was there to help a sick horse. I can't remember all the times over the years I've experienced similar situations; having something unexpected happen, something unplanned, perhaps even undesired. It's about being part of an ordinary context, being part of life on the move.

Daniel Stern describes,

> that missteps are most valuable because the manner of negotiating repairs, and correcting slippages is one of the more important ways-of-being-with-the-other that become implicitly known'. He adds, 'The rupture-repair sequence thus is one of the more important learning experiences for the infant in negotiating the imperfect world. (Stern, 2004, p. 157)

Sharing an ordinary life in a family home means both the client and the family home will make some 'missteps' as Stern calls them, saying the wrong thing at the wrong time, doing the wrong thing at the wrong time. This is part of so-called ordinary life with all its misunderstandings, shortcomings, inadequacies, and outright mistakes. Things happen in daily life that cannot always be fixed or understood, but in context with others they become comprehensible and meaning can be created out of them (Gergen, 1994).

There is a balance between, on the one hand, using ordinary language and, on the other, using therapeutic experience and knowledge. Is there a difference between them? The answer must be both yes and no. It depends on how therapeutic experience and knowledge are referred to and what is meant by ordinary language. One of my tasks as a therapist in the Extended Therapy Room is to relate to this complexity; to ask questions of myself and others as well as sometimes realizing the importance of not asking questions, but to wait in silence.

Seikkula describes the importance of listening to many voices and of letting the client and his/her family be heard. He says that one of the therapist's important tasks is to listen not only to what is being expressed verbally, but also what is wordlessly communicated (Seikkula, 2011).

In the Extended Therapy Room, the client and his/her family meet both therapists and family home members who aren't professional colleagues. They are something else. That something else affects us all and leaves its mark on the therapeutic conversation. In daily life, people don't usually take a reflective position or think in terms of transference and counter-transference. They bring themselves to a situation and what occurs could be described as a spontaneous meeting or conversation. The challenge for me as a therapist is to relate to this spontaneity and to try to be present in what is going on without knowing in advance what the conversation and meeting will be like.

This requires being open to what comes to life inside of me in the form of thoughts and bodily sensations. When I say openness, I don't mean I always have to or even should share these thoughts and feelings with the others, but I need to find a way to notice them for myself. On the other hand, there might be situations where it is essential that I as the therapist put my own experiences into words.

The therapeutic meeting is about being attentive in the sense of being present and striving together to create meaning out of what is going on. It's about listening, even to the complicated, the 'knotty,' that which is beyond words and manualized questionnaires. Bruce Wampold shows in his research why the randomized research method is insufficient for investigating the therapeutic meeting; because the unique meeting contains things that aren't easily captured in predetermined concepts or something specific the research is intended to examine. There is a risk that by being bound to one or a few variables what is most important gets lost because it can't be measured (Wampold, 2001).

Today I have the words to express this, but in the early years it wasn't articulated. At that time, the focus was on ongoing lived experience, and neither I nor others reflected from psychological or psychotherapeutic concepts or theories when we sat together at the kitchen table in the family home. The practical situation steered our conversations as well as the feelings we all sensed. Sometimes I think it was an advantage that we didn't 'know' so much, and that maybe it was a prerequisite for daring to do what we did. This therapeutic 'ignorance' together with limited therapeutic experience meant we had to rely on something else; each other and the relationship we had with each other, as well as on ourselves and what felt right or seemed to be important.

> The aspects of things that are most important for us are hidden because of their simplicity and familiarity (one is unable to notice something – because it is always before one's eyes). The real foundation of his enquiry do not strike a man at all, unless that fact has at some time struck him. And this means: we fail to be struck by what, once seen; is most striking and most powerful. (Wittgenstein, 2007, p. 129)

## To be in the middle of life's different moments

In a recent documentary about our work in the Extended Therapy Room, directed by Daniel Mackler (Healing Homes, 2011), there is a scene where the family home father, Jonas, talks about a serious and very decisive moment, and at the same time, the family home mother, Annki, shows me a new flower she'd purchased as if it was the most important thing in the moment. A moment later lightning strikes not far from the house and the lights go out. The dogs get anxious and whine for attention, their panting can be clearly heard. One of the sons comes home for a little food. The interruptions don't stop the conversation. We continue to talk, giggle a little, get sidetracked for a little while, and pick up the thread of the conversation again with the additions the interruptions created.

When watching that scene, I think about how I interpret what happens from lived experience in the Extended Therapy Room. The interruptions don't disturb anything. They rather open up and create opportunities to see more, and to hear more. The dogs pant and I think that if I hadn't experienced hundreds of hours talking in family home kitchens with panting dogs at my feet, perhaps the dogs' presence might have been a bother. But I don't feel that way because I have a lived experience concerning the importance of being surrounded by panting dogs in a family home kitchen while an important conversation or a wordless meeting takes place.

Tom Andersen described how he has made decisions based on practical situations, for example, when he as a young doctor was called to the home of a family on the night before Christmas Eve, where he had to decide whether or not to let the father stay at home or be admitted to a psychiatric hospital. Andersen gathered the family together for a conversation instead of deciding on the authority of his expertise. It was an important choice that turned out to be significant for his perspective on therapeutic work (Abrahamsson & Berglund, 2000).

## Organizations consist of human beings

One of my main tasks as a psychotherapist is to create room for meetings to take place between people. This requires a therapist's presence, but it also calls for an organization and structure where there is space for spontaneity and improvisation, where the spontaneous and unplanned is accepted and allowed. The fact that I and my colleagues were not steeped in education and were rather inexperienced therapeutically and professionally when we started the

Family Care Foundation possibly promoted spontaneity and improvisation. In addition, there were very few role models since we were pioneers in this field. We therefore had no other choice unless we wanted to follow an external book of rules, and we didn't.

> By our very attitude to one another we help to shape one another's world. By our attitude to the other person we help to determine the scope and hue of his world; we make it large or small, bright or drab, rich or dull, threatening or secure. We help to shape his world not by theories and views but by our very attitude towards him. (Lögstrup, 1971, p. 19)

For any of us in the organization, following an external book of rules has never been an option. Instead, we had to improvise and trust our own and others' lived experiences. This experience wasn't formulated in specific methods or theories, but in a number of images and lived experiences of being a human being among other human beings.

## Our work is based on practice

The Extended Therapy Room as a concept is rooted in practice. It has grown out of close collaboration between family homes, clients, their families, therapists, and other staff members. In my book *The Extended Therapy Room*, how the concept was created and articulated as a consequence of the fact that existing concepts couldn't adequately describe our work is decribed.

> We work with family care, and we offer our clients psychotherapy but the extended therapy room is not one thing or another but both. The extended therapy room symbolizes a room where family care and psychotherapy meet, inspire each other and become each other's prerequisite. Experience shows that on their own family homes and psychotherapy haven't been successful when offered to the clients that I and my colleagues meet in our work. (Håkansson, 2000, p. 10)

The work of Family Care Foundation is based on a vision of creating a way of working that would be good for people, a place where people would feel they had a place, whether they were clients, their families, professional helpers, or family homes.

In other words, our vision wasn't to create a method of treatment or produce a new theory. It was about *something else*, something that had to do with the conditions of people's lives, their dreams, hopes, and chances of creating meaning in their lives. It was about something that would give people the courage to live and promote the living part of themselves. Our vision was built on the idea that we all contribute in different ways, and that these contributions form a whole where each part is vital (Bateson, 1972). The knowledge and experience the family home has of being part of an ordinary life, with all that this entails, is of crucial importance for the development of the organization, and also for me as a therapist. For example, being in situations and questions I can't with certainty resolve, and being part of life in all its richness.

John Shotter describes how knowledge gained from ordinary life affects language and relationships. He believes that knowledge is found in people's social daily life. It is through everyday language in living life that truly important knowledge develops, rather than through theoretical formulas and constructions (Shotter, 1993, 2002).

It's about creating a place where it's possible to deliver something of oneself into the hands of another person, and to be received. This is a big responsibility and it requires that both the organization and each individual do not misuse each other, and that they disregard the existing power relationship.

> That life together with and over against one another consists in one person being delivered over to another person means that our mutual relationships are always relationships of power, the one person being more or less in the power of another person. (Lögstrup, 1971, p. 55)

## Sometimes it is very hard to understand ...

In daily practice, I sometimes recognize how hard it is to honestly understand the people I meet, each bringing their unique life story to the therapeutic meeting. I cannot fully understand how it is to be a child who already at the age of 14 has been moved around to more than 10 foster homes. Or what if feels like to be forcibly injected on a psychiatric ward without realizing what is happening. Or how it is to be unable to see your parents due to their emotional condition, and carrying a feeling that it is all one's own fault. Or what it is like as a child to flee from your own country and to rely on foreigners in a place far away from everyone and everything you used to know. I need to bear that I cannot fully understand and accept there are no manual-based formulas or theories in the world which makes me fully understand either. At the same time, I cannot give up the idea of trying together with those whom it concerns to make some sense of what is happening.

As already discussed, Family Care Foundation was created as a reaction towards a system which does not take into enough consideration the many different aspects of being a human amongst other human beings. On the contrary, people become 'patients' when entering the psychiatric ward with its diagnoses, medication, and different ways of 'treating' the person, as if their way of behaving is a symptom of an illness and something which it is not possible to make sense of.

## That which is important in life and in therapy

As a young social worker, I was fortunate enough to meet with two devoted and skilled therapists who cooperated with engaged and life-experienced family homes. Immediately I fell in love with the commitments, the openness, and, above all, the authenticity, which was very present, not only regarding the family homes, but also regarding the professional helpers. This, I felt, was something I wanted to learn more about and to be part of

(Håkansson, 2014). Many years have passed since then, but what was important at the time remains most important: to find a way together with others to create a space where people are invited, where they can have a sense of feeling safe and the chance to make sense of what is happening to them now or in the past.

Tom Andersen used to describe life as a project, the purpose of which is to find out how to move from one moment to the next. He compared this life process with the therapeutic process – in therapy as in life, one has to follow that which happens in the moment (Andersen, 1996, 2011). I would like to add that in order to make sense of what is happening right now, it has to be related to something that has happened in the past. One's own lived experience but also the other's lived experience, which together create the possibility of making sense of what is happening right now, in life as in the therapeutic meeting. It does not mean that life is predetermined, rather the opposite as lived experience as well as therapeutic knowledge illustrate in many ways how impossible it is to know beforehand what will happen to us.

As important as the past might be, a person's impulse towards growth and change is also important, and here is where the therapist and the therapy play an essential role.

Jessie Taft, a pioneer in social work and therapy, said;

> The basic need of the individual, after all, is not pleasure but more life, to make more and more of the underlying energy accessible for integration, to go with the life process instead of fighting it, and to find and use his own capacity for relationships and for creativity, however slight. Pleasure, or better said, satisfaction, attends the active, successful expression of the organized will; it is a by-product, not a motive or an end in itself. (Robinson, 1962, p. 336)

In Taft's writing, I recognize something from my workplace, but it is also reminiscent of Barbro Sandin's work. At the end of 1970s, she started something which in the Swedish newspapers was described as 'a revolution,' when she stated there is no such thing as schizophrenia as an illness, but rather as a reaction to something too difficult to deal with.

Sandin devoted her life and work to people labeled with 'schizophrenia' and she did not ever give up the idea that what was defined as an illness may have more to do with life conditions and relationships. Sandin's focus in therapeutic work is on relationships: between therapist and client, as well as the clients' relationship to herself, her history, and context.

Sandin's understanding of psychotic conditions is based on knowledge about children's natural development and how this can be disrupted. In therapeutic practice, Sandin shows the necessity of creating a connection between the therapist and the client, a recreation of the early loss of actual relationships and the sense of one's own self. She shows the importance of being present, of having the patience to wait, and of listening to what is said and what is felt in the body. And when it is time, to help create a language and let the words be significant for meaning creation (Sandin, 1986; Sandin, Haugsgjerd, Nergård, & Rossvaer, 1990).

## The increasing number of diagnoses and different approaches

In 1933, Taft writes;

> In the last analysis, therapy as a qualitative affair must depend on the personal development of the therapist and his ability to use consciously for the benefit of his client, the insight and self-discipline he has achieved in his own struggle to accept self, life, and time as limited, and to be experienced fully only at the cost of fear, pain and loss. I do not mean that knowledge is not necessary, that technical skill is not necessary; they are, but they are of no value therapeutically without the person. To make casework therapeutic, incidentally or deliberately, one must be a therapist and only to that extent that this is true are the relationships one sets up therapeutic, regardless of the label, the number of the visits, or the interpretation recorded in the dictation. (Taft, 1933)

Many years have passed since then, but the message is still very radical and a challenge for practice today with the increasing variety of methods, psychotherapeutic approaches, models, and 'solutions' that it is tempting to define it as an epidemic. Robert Whitaker describes a similar phenomenon due to psychiatric diagnosis and the skyrocketing use of pharmaceutical drugs during the last decades (Whitaker, 2010).

When examining research into psychology and psychotherapy, it is striking how frequently the word 'treatment' is used. This is a trend which appears to have started in the middle of 1980s, at a time when manual-based formulae were introduced to a wider public. In addition, to a large extent, research focuses on 'how to find the best treatment' and how to create methods that allow for comparative research between different treatments and different patients. Still the question remains, how does one use this knowledge?

Similarly, research has taken place for decades at a cost of billions of dollars to prove the causes of 'schizophrenia' and 'ADHD' (two examples of psychiatric diagnosis), as Whitaker describes in his book (Whitaker, 2010).

So far has no one managed to prove *why* people feel the way they do, why do some people react in one way and others in another way. In her autobiography, Jeanette Winterson writes,

> As I try and understand how life works – and why some people cope better than others with adversity – I come back to something that has to do with saying yes to life, which is love of life, however inadequate, and love for the self, however found. Not in the me – first way that is the opposite of life and love, but with a salmon-like determination to swim upstream, however choppy upstream is, because this is your stream … (Winterson, 2010, p. 24)

## What is most important?

Working as a therapist, I have asked myself many times over the years what is important in the therapeutic meeting, and what part do I as a psychotherapist play in that? In what way do I and my way of *being-in-the-world* (Heidegger, 1962) contribute to what unfolds in the meeting with the other?

Regardless of whether we are called therapists, family homes, or clients, we are affected by each other and the situations we find ourselves in. We bear with us our personal history while we are also part of a larger context. Those of us working as psychotherapists have the potential to contribute with knowledge about human beings and human life conditions, due to the fact that we more than most people participate in conversations about human life and life dilemmas.

Jessie Taft describes in her writing how the fear of emotions can make us vulnerable, and she links it to the fact that feelings so often are denied and feared, or even condemned, by scientists as well as by practitioners. In her opinion, this attitude originates in a complete misunderstanding of emotions and their role in life (Taft, 1933). Taft asks how to deal with emotions in therapeutic work, a question which is maybe even more relevant today than 80 years ago, since it seems far too many professional helpers have given up on the importance of relationships and instead focus on 'how to find the right method and the right treatment.'

Taft describes the essence of being met as a real person by another real person. She proposes that the child does not need perfectly understanding parents, as the client does not need the perfectly understanding therapist, but instead contact with living, responsive, and changing persons who are not afraid of their own or others' feelings.

In a similar way, Barbro Sandin, my mentor for many years, describes her therapeutic work with people who had withdrawn from life, and were isolated and filled with fear. It was not through a specific approach, method, or manual that she was helpful to the person in need. Rather, it was by being there and finding a way together with the other to slowly, piece by piece, link him to a connected reality (Sandin, 1986; Sandin et al., 1990).

One of the main findings in my thesis was to acknowledge the importance of including oneself and one's lived experience in the therapeutic meeting. To recognize a therapeutic mindset that differs from so-called therapeutic neutrality and objectivity. The work described is affected by close collaboration with so-called 'ordinary people' – those in family homes as well as clients and their families, colleagues, and an extensive network.

It is not based on a medical model founded on the concept of measurable objective knowledge, but on the importance of subjective experience, my lived experience in a context together with others.

Having participated in collaborative work in the Extended Therapy Room over the years, I have discovered the importance of meeting authentic people in different situations; in the therapy room, during a team meeting, in a family home kitchen, during a car ride. The family home members have taught me the essence of therapy, which is to be there together with the other one, to dare to trust that which is happening in the moment, to experience there are no 'right' ways to connect with another human being, but rather to dare to follow that which happens, and to be authentic.

It is not easily done, and I experienced hours and hours of doubts, fear, anxiety, questioning, and a feeling of not knowing. I have found the importance of holding on to some frames, for example, time as a limit, team work, and to be part of a living organization. Responsibility and power, my own and others, are essential issues to be dealt with and to work with continuously, by one self and together with others. Mentorship is essential, to lean on other people's wisdom and lived experience, and to learn from their thoughts, ideas, and theoretical dilemmas. It is not necessary to find a therapist as a mentor, but rather someone who is present in the meeting, someone who has taken a personal stance and is willing to be part of something that is not always possible to describe verbally, but rather by emotions together with wonderings about what is happening right now.

The story at the beginning of this essay illustrates how crucial it is to be met in an ordinary context without being defined by psychiatric language, but rather as someone who has a lot of different skills, dreams, and difficulties. The family home created together by the family as well as by me and my colleague offers a space where something different happens to what is written about the boy in professional files. Together, we create a space where it becomes possible to see and hear something else. Each of us contributes and each of us affects and is affected by the situation, which altogether creates a new image, a new story to be told which hopefully might change existing life conditions.

There are moments and situations, in psychotherapy as in life, that can't be proven or verbally explained, which perhaps can't be completely understood. Our shared work entails, as in life, moments of deepest fear as well as moments of wonderful joy. It is a matter of coming forth, for the therapist as well as for the family home and client, and to dare to try the unknown and to be part of an authentic meeting.

## Disclosure statement

No potential conflict of interest was reported by the author.

## References

Abrahamsson, E., & Berglund, G. (2000). *Creative conversations*. Stockholm: Mareld.

Andersen, T. (1996). *Reflecting processes: Acts of informing and forming: You can borrow my eyes, but you must not take them away from me!* Collaborative Practice in Family Therapy. New York, NY: Guilford Press.

Andersen, T. (2011). *Reflekterande processer: samtal och samtal om samtalen* [Reflecting Processes, Conversations and Conversations about the Conversations]. Lund: Studentlitteratur.

Bateson, G. (1972). *Steps to an ecology of mind*. New York, NY: Ballantine of Books.

Gergen, K. (1994). *Realities and relationships: Soundings in social construction*. Cambridge, MA: Harvard University Press.

Håkansson, C. (2009). *Ordinary life therapy – Experiences from a collaborative systemic practice*. Ohio: Taos Institute Publishers.

Håkansson, C. (2014) *The extended therapy room – Coming from an authentic place*. Jyväskylä: University of Jyväskylä.

Heidegger, M. (1962). *Being and time*. New York, NY: Harper & Row.

Lögstrup, K. E. (1971). *The ethical demand*. Philadelphia, PA: Fortress Press.

Mackler, D. (2011). *Healing Homes*. New York, NY: Wild Truth.

Robinson, V. (1962). *Jessie Taft: Therapist and social work educator: A professional biography*. Philadelphia, PA: University of Pennsylvania Press.

Sandin, B. (1986). *Den zebrarandiga pudelkärnan* [The Poodles Zebra-striped soul]. Stockholm: Wahlström & Widstrand.

Sandin, B., Haugsgjerd, S., Nergård, J.-I., & Rossvaer, V. (1990). *Barbro Sandins disputation*. Stockholm: Rabén & Sjögren.

Seikkula, J. (2011). *Becoming dialogical: Psychotherapy or a way of life*. Richmond, VA: AAFT, The Australian and New Zealand Journal of Psychotherapy.

Shotter, J. (1993). *Cultural politics of everyday life: Social constructionism, rhetoric and knowing of the third kind*. Milton Keynes: Milton Keynes Open University Press.

Shotter, J. (2002). *Conversational realities – Construction life through Language*. London: Sage.

Stern, D. (2004). *The present moment in psychotherapy and everyday life*. New York, NY: W.W. Norton & Company.

Taft, J. (1933). *The dynamics of therapy in a controlled relationship*. Philadelphia, PA: The MacMillan Company.

Wampold, B. E. (2001). *The great psychotherapy debate. Models, methods and findings*. London: Lawrence Earlbaum.

Whitaker, R. (2010). *Anatomy of an epidemic: Magic bullets, psychiatric drugs, and the astonishing rise of mental illness in America*. New York, NY: Crown Publishing Group, Broadway Paperback.

Winterson, J. (2010). *Why be happy when you could be normal*. New York, NY: Grove Press.

Wittgenstein, L. (2007). *Philosophical investigations*. Oxford: Blackwell Publishing.

# From victimhood to sisterhood – A practice-based reflexive inquiry into narrative informed group work with women who have experienced sexual abuse

Leah Salter

This paper will present some of the relational contexts and considerations of a female therapist's role within an island community group for women who have shared experiences of abuse and injustice; her relationship to the group, to her systemic and narrative practices; and to the research that has ensued. Exploring the changing relational contexts as the group moves from a facilitator led to a peer support group; and the associated language shifts from a binary discourse of 'other than' to a collective definition of 'sisterhood' is part of the story, which also includes the important themes of community engagement, social action and the complexities of insider/practice-based research.

Der vorliegende Artikel legt einige der relationalen Kontexte und Gesichtspunkte einer weiblichen Therapeutenrolle offen, die aus ihrer Arbeit mit einer Gruppe von Frauen resultieren, die die Erfahrung von Missbrauch und Ungerechtigkeit machen mussten; ihre Beziehungen zu der Gruppe, zu ihrer systemischen und narrativen Praxis und zu der Forschung, die sich daraus ergab. Zudem wird untersucht, wie sich die relationalen Kontexte verändert haben, als die Gruppe sich von einer moderierten Gruppe hin zu einer Peergroup entwickelte; und die damit verbundenen Veränderungen in der Sprache sind ebenfalls Teil des Artikels: von binären Diskussionen im Sinne eines 'mit Ausnahme von' hin zu einer kollektiven Definition von 'Schwesternschaft'; er beinhaltet zudem die wichtigen Themen: Engagements in der Gemeinschaft, soziales Handeln und der Komplexität von Teilnehmern und praxisbasierter Forschung.

Este artículo presenta algunos de los contextos relacionales y consideraciones del role de una mujer terapeuta dentro de un grupo comunitario de mujeres en una isla, las cuales han compartido experiencias de abuso e injusticia; su relación con el grupo, con su práctica narrativa y sistémica y con la investigación subsecuente. Se explora el cambio en el contexto relacional cuando el grupo pasa de ser un grupo guiado por un facilitador a un grupo de apoyo entre iguales; los cambios en el lenguaje asociados con el paso de un discurso binario "éste o aquél" hacia una definición colectiva de solidaridad como parte de la historia; ésta también incluye los temas importantes de compromiso con la comunidad, acción social y las complejidades de una investigación basada en la práctica desde dentro del grupo.

Questo contributo intende presentare alcuni contesti relazionali di un gruppo-comunità per donne che hanno subito esperienze di abusi e ingiustizie, oltre che considerazioni sul ruolo del terapeuta donna all'interno del gruppo, il suo rapporto con il gruppo, le pratiche sistemiche e narrative utilizzate e la ricerca che ne è seguita. Esplorare come cambiano i contesti relazionali, come il gruppo si sposta da una conduzione da parte del facilitatore ad un sostegno tra pari; i movimenti nell'uso del linguaggio da un duplice "diverso da" ad una definizione collettiva di "sorellanza" dentro la storia, che comprende anche gli importanti temi di coinvolgimento della comunità, l'azione sociale e le difficoltà relative all'esser membro del gruppo e alla ricerca basata sulla pratica.

Cet article présente certains des contextes relationnels et les considérations du rôle d'une femme thérapeute au sein d'un groupe émanant d'une communauté insulaire pour des femmes ayant partagé leurs expériences de l'abus et de l'injustice ; sa relation au groupe, ses pratiques systémiques et narratives et la recherche qui s'en est suivie. Explorant les contextes relationnels se modifiant à mesure que le groupe passe d'un groupe mené par un facilitateur à un groupe d'entraide entre pairs ; et les modifications du langage associées d'un 'autre que' à une définition collective de 'solidarité féminine' qui font parties de l'histoire ; et qui inclut également les thèmes importants de l'engagement au sein de la communauté, de l'action sociale et des complexités de la recherche interne/ fondée sur la pratique.

Αυτό το άρθρο θα παρουσιάσει μερικά από τα σχεσιακά πλαίσια και τις σκέψεις μιας γυναίκας θεραπεύτριας από το ρόλο της μέσα σε μια νησιωτική κοινοτική ομάδα με γυναίκες που έχουν βιώσει εμπειρίες κακοποίησης και αδικίας· από τη σχέση της με την ομάδα, τις συστημικές και αφηγηματικές πρακτικές και την έρευνα που ακολούθησε. Μελετώνται τα μεταβαλλόμενα σχεσιακά πλαίσια , καθώς η ομάδα πέρασε από το να εμψυχώνεται από ια συντονίστρα στο να γίνει ομάδα αλληλοϋποστήριξης. Μελετώνται επίσης σχετικές αλλαγές στη γλώσσα από ένα δυαδικό λόγο «είτε/ ή» σε έναν συλλογικό ορισμό της «αδελφότητας», που είναι μέρος της ιστορίας, η οποία περιλαμβάνει επίσης τα σημαντικά θέματα της εμπλοκής στην κοινότητα, της κοινωνικής δράσης και την συνθετότητα που διέπει την έρευνα που γίνεται «εκ των έσω» και βασίζεται στη μελέτη της πρακτικής.

## Introduction

### *Prologue*

I first presented a draft version of this paper as a 'work in progress' at the Taos Conference in Drammen, Norway in 2014 but since then I have begun the 'fieldwork' element of my doctoral inquiry which focuses on 'going on' after groups I have set up and been part of. My conversations with co-facilitators of those groups have already significantly shifted my thinking. Some extracts from those conversations are included in this paper as examples of practice and research issues.

This paper represents a reflexive inquiry into my own practices and it is part of a wider Narrative Inquiry, where I will be inquiring into stories of 'going on' after groups I have been part of. This will include my own experiences (some of which are highlighted here) and will include conversations with women who have been part of groups I have facilitated. This is all still in progress, and I have just started this process by having conversations with colleagues. As such my relationship to this paper and my ideas around 'what makes research, research' are still in development. This paper represents a marker along the way of the journey and an opportunity to reflect on my own developing research practices. It also offers an opportunity to highlight some important ethical issues within a frame of 'relational responsibility' (McNamee & Gergen, 1999) and 'social justice'; set within a wider social constructionist context.

## Methodology

### *Adopting autoethnography*

By adopting more of an autoethnographic lens in this paper, I hope to foreground the connections with my own story, the influences on my practice and my relationship to this particular group.

Ellis (2004) defines autoethnography as 'research, writing, story, and method that connect the autobiographical and personal to the cultural, social and political'. It is an approach to research and writing that foregrounds personal and cultural experiences, including the researcher's own experiences, which are 'brought forth' to recognise the influence on the research. The autoethnographer positions herself centrally, not to be self-indulgent but to offer a 'political, socially-just and socially-conscious' method (Ellis, 2004) as an alternative to other modes of inquiry that may amplify hierarchical differences between 'researcher' and 'researched'. Autoethnography is often criticised for being too focused on the individual, notably the researcher (see e.g. Atkinson, 1997; Coffey, 1999) and for focusing on the therapeutic rather than analytic value of research (Atkinson, 1997; Walford, 2004). 'Relational ethnography', with an embedded invitation to focus more fully on relationships, goes some way to address that critique. Gail Simon suggests that *relational* ethnography foregrounds reflexivity and dialogical practices and offers a mode of inquiry that speaks 'about *and from within* relationships' (Simon, 2013, p. 11).

### *Relational ethics*

Etherington (2003, 2004) describes writing personal stories as becoming 'agents in our own lives' and reclaiming a voice that might previously have been marginalised or silenced because of experiences that have been 'culturally denied.' (Etherington, 2003, p. 20) For me, this is part of the relational dance between my story of selfhood/womanhood, my practices, my inquiry and my contributions to social justice, what Gail Simon may refer to as 'praction research.' (Simon, 2012, 2014)

Foregrounding the role of social action in feminist research, Lather (1991) argues that research needs to go 'beyond the concern for more and better data to a concern for research as praxis … to use our research to help participants understand and change their situations.' Lather (1991, p. 57)

I am influenced by feminist research and the relational ethnographic invitation to reclaim my own voice to contribute to social justice. Taking up that invitation, I started writing a journal and practising saying aloud some of my previously undeclared stories of selfhood/womanhood as a means to perform my own stories of injustice. This is part of an ethical position to challenge objectification of women as 'victims' of abuse. I highlight my story to not only challenge that assumption of 'victimhood' but also to enable the reader to hear the voice of the author as not just an objective narrator, but as integral to the relational narrative of practice-based research.

### *From third to first person*

Though autoethnographic narratives may be written in third or first person (see Mendez, 2013 for further detail) writing in the first person for me supports personal and relational reflexivity and crucially helps to protect anonymity by naming myself, rather than others. I am also intentionally moving away from a style of reading, writing and practice that can hold people (often unintentionally) in an objectified position. Writing in this way affords me that same respect, avoiding being reduced to a singular definition of self as 'author'. I am offering here multiple definitions of self, as a practitioner, as a researcher, an island resident and a woman who has her own stories of injustice. The influence of Wittgenstein (1953) should be made visible here in foregrounding ideas of 'going on'. I am referring here to relationally oriented ways of being that enable me/us to speak outside of definitions of, for example, 'victimhood'. I aim to bring singular, restraining definitions of relationship into question whether they are in relation to me, or others.

## Going on

### *Lending my own voice*

As a woman influenced by feminist methodologies, and a psychotherapist working predominantly with women I have chosen to foreground my own gender here. I have also chosen to use both first names and surnames when referring to significant influences on my practice as a means to make gender visible in my research practice.

As someone who has lived and worked in different parts of the British Isles, I choose also to highlight my cultural heritage as part of my identity. The more I have travelled, the more curious I have become about how my own cultural and personal experiences have shaped me. I come from a fairly large Welsh docks town which can be described as predominantly white and working class, which is part of my heritage. This 'classing', as with other cultural markers is not static. For example, I had a fairly average state education and left school without too much direction before finding my way (eventually) to further education and becoming an avid learner and teacher, which has somewhat changed my 'status'. My cultural experiences have also changed. My working life as a Systemic Psychotherapist has predominantly been based in small semi-rural communities, which represents personal and professional changes.

Some of the women in my inquiry have a similar cultural heritage to my own, some do not; but all of them have experience of being part of a small community, which in this inquiry has been a visible contextual and relational marker. Some are mothers, some are not. I am married, without children, so I do not share some of their shared experiences of parenthood. This can be a platform for rich conversations about family life and differences, and represents another relational marker.

Of course there are other unique stories that I do not share, but some that I do. I have my own stories to tell of power and powerlessness. One of these stories I share with some friends from my home town; our experience of a music teacher who was subsequently convicted of child sex abuse. Though I have had very few conversations about this since and do not know the detail of others' stories, I do know that I was lucky enough to be believed, which limited the abuse *and* its impact, whereas other children were less fortunate. Chesler (2005) tells us that '… women and men can survive many things – if they are believed, if others are outraged on their behalf …'. This notion is reflected not only in my personal and professional story, but in the stories that women have shared with me in therapy and in this group. I do consider that I survived my experience but I would not label myself as a 'victim' or a 'survivor' of that experience. These words do not pay enough attention to the multiple and complex relationships that are inherent in stories of abuse which are far more complex than words like 'perpetrator' or 'victim' suggest. I do however remain 'outraged' about injustice and this is part of how I 'go on'.

I made the decision not to disclose my story to the women in the group, in order to protect myself/my professional identity in this small community; and to protect other women in the group from any sense of responsibility towards me. Roberts's (2005) paper on the 'dangers and possibilities' of transparency in therapy cites feedback from a client who had that very experience, highlighting the risks as well as potential gains for therapists sharing stories from their lives outside of the therapy room.

My own view is that making transparent conceptual models born from training or personal experience (see e.g. Andersen, 1987; White, 1995) is a helpful, ethical position for the therapist/ group facilitator to take, but sharing personal stories that may indicate potential trauma is far more complex. These stories can impact negatively on the relationship and on the person in therapy. These kinds of decisions remain at the forefront of my thinking in my ongoing research, bringing to centre stage the question of power and choice in the research as well as therapeutic context.

### *Power and choice*

Choices about 'telling' or 'not telling', whether in therapy, in research or in less defined conversational spaces, can create very real tensions in small communities that are largely 'self-referential' and invest heavily in maintaining the status quo. Research into these sensitive subjects in a highly sensitised community is complex. I, perhaps like other people who begin research as a practitioner within the community they are writing about, have found myself moving from a 'holder' of stories towards a 'sharer' of stories and with this comes a particular responsibility. As such I have needed to make certain choices about how I go on. One of the decisions I have made is to not only anonymise the women I will be talking with (group members) but also anonymise the communities we are part of. This is not unheard of in ethnographic research, as a means to protect identities and as part of a responsibility to relational ethics. (Ellis, 2011; Fine, 1993) *But* it involves compromise, including not foregrounding particular cultural stories/nuances that might pinpoint this particular community. However, it enables me to continue to practice and live ethically within the community. The women in the group have also made similar compromises that enable them to go on living and working in their island home.

Below is an extract from a conversation between myself and two colleagues, Janey and Lucy, both working in the health service. We have all facilitated groups for women who have experienced sexual abuse at different stages of the life/legacy of 'the group'. Janey was part of the original development, Lucy and I the more recent. The extract highlights the reticence we all faced in continuing, amidst vocalised angst about 'opening a can of worms' which was voiced at both a clinical and political level.

Me: Do you think that was like a multi layered thing cos I looking back … I wonder whether it wasn't just that you are opening a can of worms for that one individual (and that we need to check that that individual is safe) but I wonder also if … whether there was a sense … that we might be uncovering something that would be better off covering up (at a societal level)?

Janey: (emphatically) yes …. I was thinking that just now really, I was thinking that if you look at the evidence base in terms of how many people are likely to have experienced sexual abuse who also experience mental health issues in adulthood, it's umm quite shocking the absence of service for those groups of people, and you wonder if the service is actually reflecting society's wish …

## *Withness*

The interpretative turn, as it has become known, in the 1980s highlights the shift from objective/objectifying, anthropological research 'about' communities and cultures to an invitational stance for people of all cultures and communities to interpret meaning in their own lives.

Shotter (2005, 2011) might refer to this shift as being a move from 'aboutness' thinking to 'withness' thinking. White and Epston (1990) might note this shift as significant in the development of Narrative Therapy and in Narrative research, foregrounding collaboration between the therapist and 'client' as co-researchers in a personal and relational inquiry. The invitation to question social injustices is highlighted here by Michael White in a previously unpublished paper, published posthumously in 2011.

> Is it our role to be the unwitting accomplices of modern power, or is it our role to sponsor diversity in everyday life? Is it our role to promote single-storied conceptions of life – or to bring forth complexity in the sense of alternative stories of life? Is the therapy room a context for the confirmation of the known and familiar, or is it a context for arriving at what it might be possible to know? Is it a context for domesticating the exotic, or is it a context for 'exoticizing' the domestic? White (2011, p. 43)

## *Doing withness*

Whilst I have chosen not to name the women I will be talking with in this inquiry, I aim to actively position myself as being alongside other women from the group within the (relational) ethics of 'solidarity' and 'justice-doing' (Reynolds, 2010, 2014) and within the frame of 'withness' thinking (Shotter, 1999, 2005, 2011). As such I am actively using my voice and personal experiences to speak out about stories of injustice, whilst continuing to listen to the women I am talking with.

Reynolds (2014) describes this relational positioning as an 'imperfect alliance'. The women I am talking with are the experts on their own lives and experiences, and my role, as I see it, is to position myself ethically in relation to their story and expertise, so as to notice and highlight stories of competence and of 'going on' outside of the language of psychopathology and 'victimhood'.

McNamee (2009) calls this being 'relationally engaged' in a context of 'radical constructivism' and within the ethics of 'relational responsibility' (McNamee & Gergen, 1999). I have started to refer to this as 'doing withness' as a way of denoting the active process of 'being with' that extends outside of the therapy room. For me, this suggests a sense of movement and action beyond 'being with', contributing to a wider political agenda of co-creating better 'social worlds' (Pearce, 2007).

It is my intention therefore by inquiring into, and then writing about these important stories, to offer 'witness' (White, 1995, 2000, 2007); 'withness' (Shotter, 1999, 2005, 2011) and a platform to social justice. This is my aim, but friction still remains in the mix. Finding the right kind of fit in terms of methodology has been part of that tussle.

### *Relational reflexivity*

> Self-reflexivity is an essential component for unsettling hierarchies in the feminist research project. The text becomes a co-constructed space that reveals the interaction between the researcher's assumptions and positionality and the voices, stories and experiences of the research subjects. Consequently, the ethnographic text ... is the outcome of the embodied, lived experience of fieldwork. Nencel (2013, p. 76)

*Relational* reflexivity is integral to practice-based research. As I write I am conscious of the recursive movement within and between different learning 'zones' (Vygotsky, 1978) of 'writing about what I have learnt' and 'learning as I write'. The process of writing has the effect of moving me on in my thinking and in my practice. This brings us back to Gail Simon's concept of 'praction research' where writing is a form of inquiry and the Systemic researcher is inherently engaged in social justice. (Simon, 2012, 2014) This is a similar process to the one that plays out in therapy and in groups. Speaking out loud one's story has a forming and a transforming quality, allowing new stories to emerge, through the telling, sharing and 'witnessing' (White, 1995, 2000, 2007).

The following excerpt from Richardson (1990) sums up why, as a Systemic Psychotherapist, I might be interested in working with groups *and* why I might invest my own resources into researching such relational experiences.

> By emotionally binding together people who have had the same experiences, the collective story overcomes some of the isolation and alienation of contemporary life. It provides a sociological community, the linking of separate individuals into a shared consciousness. Once linked, the possibility for social action on behalf of the collective is present, and, therewith, the possibility of social transformation.
> Richardson (1990)

### *Narrative influences*

Narrative Therapy (Denborough, 2008, 2014; Freedman & Combs, 1996; White, 2000; White & Epston, 1990) highlights the 'transformative' function in storying lived experience through the performance of relationship; and the 'witnessing' of stories (White, 1995, 2000, 2007; White & Epston, 1990). 'Witnessing' is not a passive act of observation but a dynamic act of co-creating a space where new and evolving stories can emerge, often involving other people from the community. My view is that the group experience allows for a similar space to be co-created where 'preferred futures' are generated (Denborough, 2008, 2014; White, 1995; White & Epston, 1990). This is further mirrored in the research relationship as new stories emerge in the present in what could be otherwise described as a retrospective, reflective process. This is inherently connected to ideas around legacy and succession embedded in narrative practices, allowing future possibilities to open up in the process of talking about multigenerational cultural narratives. As a practitioner-researcher 'doing withness' means that I can be with people who have experienced injustice when we are in dialogue together *and* when in dialogue with others through the process of writing. John Shotter refers to this as 'withness writing' (Shotter, 1999, 2005, 2011), inviting dialogue through the process of writing and reading. Gail Simon refers to this as speaking and writing from 'within relationship' (Simon, 2013).

Connelly and Clandinin (2013) note the significance of the relationship between inquirer and co-researcher in narrative inquiry also as a catalyst for emerging stories that speak to a growing sense of community and social justice. The therapeutic nature of the group I was part of, heavily influenced by my own leanings towards Narrative approaches, encouraged and supported us all to be moved by the stories we were telling, sharing, witnessing and 'withness-ing'. This has been a significant thread in the 'going on' of the group and those who were/are part of it.

In therapy, as Anderson (1997) puts it, both client and therapist 'risk' change, a relational view of change as happening 'between'. This rings true for the relationship between practitioner-researcher and co-researchers, and I would suggest that communities too 'risk' change when women come together and generate stories of social justice. There is considerable risk here for all involved, not least because by the very act of attending the women are 'outing' themselves as having experienced sexual abuse. The community also risks the possibility that the group experience of injustice may lead to community action as Connelly and Clandinin (2013) suggest.

### *Mapping the context*

The island community within which I work and live has a particular history of 'naming and shaming'. The local newspaper thrives on stories and pictures of people who have veered from the local laws and cultural rules such as stories of theft, drug use or driving under the influence of alcohol, with both the 'law-breaker' and 'victim' being named. Stories of sexual abuse however do not have the same currency. They do not usually fit with cultural stories of identity whatever the geography, but within an island context they can have particular resonance, given the likely scenario that those who have been abused and those that abuse are likely to be living in close proximity. They are not the unknown 'other'; they are relatives, neighbours and colleagues. These stories often stand in stark contrast to the stories that people tell themselves and others about their community and family. The public nature of a disclosure therefore is an unsettling prospect; as this further example from my conversation with my colleagues illustrates.

> Janey: I feel as an outsider .... I feel as if there is ... mm ... a strong 'group think' ... that we ... are luckier than people who have to live somewhere else, and that not much bad stuff happens here compared with what happens if you live somewhere else, and to actually ... then be exposed to the fact that bad things are happening to people (quite a lot) in this community is hard because it goes against the 'group think' ...

Our experience suggests to us that women in closed communities like small islands are often holding unvoiced narratives of oppression, especially if they have been sexually abused and 'encouraged' not to tell. This community is strongly influenced by narratives about not 'rocking the boat' and wider societal discourses of women as 'victims'.

### *The language of power/power of language*

> We are not outside observers of the world. Nor are we simply located at particular places in the world; rather, we are part of the world in its ongoing intra-activity.
> Barad (2003, p. 828)

Maturana (1988) refers to the notion of observer as the 'praxis of living in language'.

To pay attention to language from a social constructionist position is to pay attention to language as 'forming' rather than purely 'informing' existing concepts.

As such language is not a 'truth-bearing' reflection of a represented world, but is constructed within social and cultural meaning. Language has the dual function of not merely describing, but also sustaining societal, cultural discourse, which can also prevent or subjugate other discourses (Foucault, 1973; Gergen, 1999). Patti Lather asserts that language is the 'terrain where differently privileged discourses struggle via confrontation and/or displacement' (Lather, 1991, p. 8).

Working within mental health services, a field that has been shaped by the language of psychopathology, I am involved in this struggle daily and try to maintain a position of 'curiosity' (Cecchin, 1987) when faced with the strength of such a discourse.

McNamee (2009) reminds us of the inherent 'problem' of diagnosis being focused on the individual which propagates the notion that 'problems' are located *within* the person. 'Labeled with their diagnosis, any hope to be "normal" is lost by virtue of being identified as flawed, inferior, unhealthy'. (McNamee, 2009)

In the specific context of sexual abuse, the language of diagnosis is ever-present, whether it be the psychiatric language of 'personality disorder' or the psychological language of 'complex trauma'. This is inherently connected with experiences of power and powerlessness, when the power to diagnose is part of the definition of relationship. Within a 'therapeutic state' (Szasz, 1984), relational ethics can easily get lost within individualised, medicalised discourses.

At a *societal* level though the language that has become ultimately 'reified' is the language of 'victimhood'. This points to a binary definition of male as perpetrator and female as victim, with inherent descriptions of power and powerlessness that need examining more closely. (See e.g. Dale, 1999; Davies & Frawley, 1994; Haaken & Schlaps, 1991)

Whilst definitions of 'victim', 'survivor' or 'thriver' can be helpful for some, my personal and professional experiences lead me to question the assumptions embedded in the language and literature. In particular, the assumption that there is a linear process to work through that includes specific stages such as 're-claiming' memories and 're-parenting the inner child'; with the ultimate aim to 'thrive'. (Bass & Davis, 1988; Parkes, 1990).

### *Legacies*

Rather than viewing 'going on' after experiences of abuse as a linear process which can hold people in an 'other than' position (i.e. 'victim' vs. 'survivor', 'survivor of sexual abuse' vs. 'normal'); I have found it more helpful to think in terms of multifaceted legacies of abuse. With intrafamilial abuse 'going on' has extra meaning given that those that have been abused by a family member not only have their trust shattered, but often live with the fear that they might have 'inherited' the genetic legacy of the abuser, that they may also go on to abuse. These worries are often the subject for difficult and painful conversations in therapy.

### *A gendered discourse*

A dominant theme for many of the women in this group, myself included, was/is women talking to women, making connections with each other and bringing cultural stereotypes into question. Using images and stories from magazines and books was part of that process, as a means to engage with ideas from different cultures, whilst deconstructing cultural stereotypes of womanhood.

The language of sisterhood 'emerged' from this context and was a word first used by one of the women who owned this as her experience of being part of the group. My understanding of 'sisterhood' (as it came to be defined in this context) was one of connectivity and solidarity. This word formed part of a new repertoire that speaks to emerging stories of 'preferred futures' outside of the language of psychopathology. (White, 1995; White & Epston, 1990)

Another example from a conversation with my colleagues may help to illustrate this further. Janey, a senior mental health practitioner and lecturer, is talking about her own journey from seeing people in a frame of what might be called 'patienthood' to one of 'personhood'. This mirrors the journey within the group of the changing language of 'victimhood' to 'sisterhood'. Binary definitions of 'them' and 'us' are also brought into question here by Lucy, a community mental health nurse, who co-facilitated the group I was part of.

Lucy: … I suppose as we all got to know each other … there became more trust in the group … we were all freed up a bit and that included 'us' not just 'them' …

Janey: … so it became less of 'us and them' and more of us all being a group of women …

Janey: … for me I've often wondered … umm … especially coming from a nursing background … you know most adult mental health nurses would have worked in inpatient settings so you … you are working with people who are really, really really unwell ummm and I've often thought that we collectively develop a defence mechanism to help us work in this way where we do regard ourselves as being 'other', 'well', 'competent', that this kind of thing wouldn't happen to us that this is the kind of thing that happens to others … they happen to 'other' people who are different to us … and for me it was part of a wider journey of considering myself as part of a human race rather than umm a 'nurse'. I am a human being the same as these other human beings and we're all in it together and you know we could all be distressed, we could all have difficulties at some point, so it required a dismantling of the defence mechanisms that have been put there for a reason and yet for me … it felt better. It felt like a better place to be …

### *Towards sisterhood*

According to Maturana (2002), our actions are structure-determined. The states of our bodyhood at any given moment are the result of the history of our living up to that moment. The meaning I take from this is that we exist in context, in relationship to what we have experienced and our interactions with others but also that we are limited within our (inter)actions within the domain of what is possible or implied by our bodily structures.

To move towards a definition of 'sisterhood' was to move within the domain of language but outside of the domain of 'victimhood', and brought a focus to the embodied, lived experiences of women. The use of mindfulness meditation within the group, exercises that involved movement and the use of gendered imagery allowed discussion about women's bodies and about embodied emotion, including pain, tears, stress and distress, without privileging a discourse of psychopathology. However, this exploration also 'lived' with the boundaries that were constructed by the context of the relationship between the women and the group. These boundaries were *both* 'determined' by the nature of how the group was set up (initially within mental health services) *and* were continuously being negotiated within the developing relationship/ interactional structures.

One way to pay attention to the transition of those relationships is/was to notice the changes in me/my role. This group has now developed into a community-based resource, with the women who have been part of the group now largely making the decisions about how to 'go on' together. Because of this change, I am no longer the 'facilitator' and I consider that I am being invited into a new relational experience. This further questions pre-suppositions of 'them' and 'us' which are bound up in the defined roles of 'facilitator' or 'referred person'.

It is early days in terms of this new development of the group as a self-directed support group and the group is still very much in transition. However, they/we are already thinking about how the group may continue to offer a supportive context for the founder members, and how it may develop to offer something to other women in the community who share similar experiences. They/we are also considering how their/our multiple voices may be heard in other contexts, and how they/we may influence change at a policy level.

## Conclusions

The group discussed in this paper and my ongoing research practice is in development so the relationship between them is constantly being re-defined and negotiated. I have though hopefully pulled together some threads of the journey thus far.

I have explored my own writing style in order to provide some context to the tone and content of the paper; and have provided several cultural reference points. The practice inquiry was offered within a frame of a first person, autoethnographic account though it represents a marker along the way of a wider Narrative Inquiry.

I have offered some reflections about the setting up of this group and its development, most notably the shift from a referred, states-run therapeutic group, to a self-directed community group. Within this, I have paid attention to the role of language, gender and community at multiple levels. I have offered the concept of 'doing withness' as a framework to my practices and intended contribution to social justice.

This has become central to my practice as systemic psychotherapist and has been foregrounded further as I move into a new role as therapist-researcher. Some of the challenges of that transition, including ethical dilemmas of transparency versus confidentiality and self-protection have also been explored.

## References

Andersen, T. (1987). The reflecting team: Dialogue and meta-dialogue in clinical work. *Family Process, 26*, 415–428.

Anderson, H. (1997). *Conversation, language and possibilities: A postmodern approach to therapy*. New York, NY: Basic Books.

Atkinson, P. (1997). Narrative turn or blind alley? *Qualitative Health Research, 7*, 325–344.

Barad, K. (2003). Posthumanist performativity: Toward an understanding of how matter comes to matter. *Journal of Women in Culture and Society, 28*(3), 801–831.

Bass, E., & Davis, L. (1988). *The courage to heal: A guide for women survivors of child sexual abuse*. New York, NY: Harper and Row.

Cecchin, G. (1987). Hypothesizing, circularity, and neutrality revisited: An invitation to curiosity. *Family Process, 26*, 405–413.

Chesler, P. (2005). *Women and madness*. New York, NY: Palgrave.

Coffey, P. (1999). *The ethnographic self*. London: Sage.

Connelly, F. M., & Clandinin, D. J. (2013). Stories of experience and narrative inquiry. *Educational Researcher, 19*, 2–14.

Dale, P. (1999). *Adults abused as children*. London: Sage.

Davies, J. M., & Frawley, M. G. (1994). *Treating the adult survivor of childhood sexual abuse: A psychoanalytic perspective*. New York, NY: Basic Books.

Denborough, D. (2008). *Collective narrative practice: Responding to individuals, groups and communities who have experienced trauma*. Adelaide: Dulwich Centre.

Denborough, D. (2014). *Retelling the stories of our lives: Everyday narrative therapy to draw inspiration and transform experience*. New York, NY: Norton.

Ellis, C. (2004). *The ethnographic I: A methodological novel about autoethnography*. Walnut Creek, CA: AltaMira Press.

Etherington, K. (2003). *Trauma, the body and transformation: A narrative inquiry*. London: Jessica Kingsley.
Etherington, K. (2004). *Becoming a reflexive researcher*. London: Jessica Kingsley.
Fine, G. (1993). Ten lies of ethnography: Moral dilemmas of field research. *Journal of Contemporary Ethnography, 22*, 267–294.
Foucault, M. (1973). *Madness and civilization*. (R. Howard, Trans.). New York, NY: Pantheon.
Freedman, J., & Combs, G. (1996). *Narrative therapy: The social construction of preferred realities*. New York, NY: Norton.
Gergen, K. (1999). *An invitation to social construction* (2nd ed.). London: Sage.
Haaken, J., & Schlaps, A. (1991). Incest resolution therapy and the objectification of sexual abuse. *Psychotherapy: Theory, Research, Practice, Training, 28*, 39–47.
Lather, P. (1991). *Getting smart: Feminist research and pedagogy with/in the postmodern*. London: Routledge.
Maturana, H. (1988). Reality. The search for objectivity or the quest for a compelling argument. *The Irish Journal of Psychology, 9*, 25–82.
Maturana, H. (2002). Autopoiesis, structural coupling and cognition: A history of these and other notions in the biology of cognition. *Cybernetics & Human Knowing, 9*, 5–34.
McNamee, S. (2009). Postmodern psychotherapeutic ethics: Relational responsibility in practice. *Human Systems: The Journal of Therapy, Consultation and Training., 20*, 57–71.
McNamee, S., & Gergen, K. J. (1999). *Relational responsibility: Resources for sustainable dialogue*. Thousand Oaks, CA: Sage.
Mendez, M. (2013). Autoethnography as a research method: Advantages, limitations and criticisms. *Colombian Applied Linguisic Journal, 15*(2), 279–287.
Nencel, L. (2013). Situating reflexivity: Voices, positionalities and representations in feminist ethnographic texts. *Women's Studies International Forum, 43*, 75–83.
Parkes, P. (1990). *Rescuing the inner child: Therapy for adults sexually abused as children*. London: Souvenir Press.
Pearce, B. (2007). *Making social worlds: A communication perspective*. Oxford: Blackwell.
Reynolds, V. (2010). *Doing justice as a path to sustainability in community work*. Retrieved November 16, 2014, from http://www.taosinstitute.net/Websites/taos/Images/PhDProgramsCompletedDissertations/ReynoldsPhDDissertationFeb2210.pdf
Reynolds, V. (2014). A solidarity approach: The rhizome and messy inquiry. In G. Simon & A. Chard (Eds.), *Systemic inquiry: Innovations in reflexive practice research*. Farnhill: Everything is connected press.
Richardson, L. (1990). *Writing strategies: Reaching diverse audiences*. London: Sage.
Roberts, J. (2005). Transparency and self-disclosure1 in family therapy: Dangers and possibilities. *Family Process, 44*, 45–63.
Shotter, J. (1999, June 3–5). Writing from within "living moments": "Withness-writing" rather than "aboutness-writing". *Fourth National Writing Across the Curriculum Conference: Multiple Intelligences*. Cornell: Cornell University.
Shotter, J. (2005). Goethe and the refiguring of intellectual inquiry: From 'aboutness'-thinking to 'withness' thinking in everyday life. *Janus Head, 8*, 132–158.
Shotter, J. (2011, March 5–9). Language, joint action, and the ethical domain: The importance of the relations between our living bodies and their surroundings. *Plenary paper to be given at III Congreso De Psicología Y Responsabilidad Social* [Congress of Psychology and Soical Responsibility]. Colombia: Campus San Alberto Magno.

Simon, G. (2012). Praction research: A model of systemic inquiry. *Human Systems Journal of Systemic Consultation and Management, 23*, 103–124.
Simon, G. (2013). Relational ethnography: Writing and reading in research relationships. *Forum: Qualitative Social Research, 14*(1), 1–13.
Simon, G. (2014). Systemic inquiry as qualitative inquiry. In G. Simon & A. Chard (Eds.), *Systemic inquiry: Innovations in reflexive practice research* (pp. 3–29). Farnhill: Everything is Connected Press.
Szasz, T. (1984). *The therapeutic state: Psychiatry in the mirror of current events*. Buffalo, NY: Prometheus Books.
Vygotsky, L. (1978). *Mind in society: The development of higher psychological processes*. Cambridge, MA: Harvard University Press.
Walford, G. (2004). Finding the limits: Autoethnography and being an Oxford University Proctor. *Qualitative Research, 4*, 403–417.
White, M. (1995). *Re-authoring lives: Interviews and essays*. Adelaide: Dulwich Centre.
White, M. (2000). *Reflections on narrative practice*. Adelaide: Dulwich Centre.
White, M. (2007). *Maps of narrative practice*. London: Norton.
White, M. (2011). *Narrative practice: Continuing the conversations*. New York, NY: Norton.
White, M., & Epston, D. (1990). *Narrative means to therapeutic ends*. New York, NY: W. W. Norton.
Wittgenstein, L. (1953). *Philosophical investigations*. Oxford: Blackwell.

# Psychotherapy and its alternatives: Commentary on a critique

Michael Rustin

In this commentary, Michael Rustin reviews the articles in the symposium, outlining their main aims and arguments. He goes on to provide some critical reflections, asking questions about the key concept of the 'therapeutic state'. He that little attention is given to psychoanalytic or other psychological theories of the mind, as distinct from the biological models which are the main object of criticism in the symposium. He argues that just as it is justifiable and useful to take account of theories of the mind in considering issues of mental health and therapy, so it is desirable also to take account of the structures of society which have responsibility for generating conditions of mental well- or ill-being, and to reflect on how these may be changed. The commentary argues that the counter-cultural and somewhat 'post-modern' critical approach which informs the symposium can only form part of a sufficient response to the problems which the symposium identifies.

Der vorliegende Kommentar fasst zunächst die wichtigsten Ziele und Argumente der Tagungsbeiträge zusammen. Im Anschluss daran wird das Schlüsselkonzept des sogenannten "Therapiestaats" einer kritischen Betrachtung unterzogen und Fragen daran gestellt. Der Kommentar stellt dabei fest, dass den psychoanalytischen oder psychologischen Theorien nur wenig Aufmerksamkeit zukommt, wohingegen die biologistischen Modelle Hauptziel der Kritik sind. Darüber hinaus, so das weitere Argument, ist es berechtigt und hilfreich, Theorien des Geistes für Aspekte der psychischen Gesundheit und Therapie heranzuziehen. Es ist jedoch in gleichem Maße erstrebenswert, die Strukturen einer Gesellschaft und deren Verhältnisse zu analysieren und zu überlegen, wie diese möglicherweise verändert werden könnten. Der Kommentar legt zudem dar, dass der subkulturelle und gewissermaßen kritisch-postmoderne Ansatz, der dem Symposium zugrunde liegt, nur teilweise eine hinreichende Antwort auf die Probleme bietet, die die Tagungsteilnehmer identifizieren.

En este comentario Michael Rustin revisa los artículos del symposium esbozando sus principales metas y discusiones, y nos da algunas reflexiones críticas haciendo preguntas acerca del concepto de ''estado terapéutico''. Según él, se ha prestado poca atención a algunas de las teorías psicológicas de la mente incluyendo al psicoanálisis, como siendo diferentes de los modelos biológicos, los cuales son el objeto principal de la crítica en el symposium. Dice que, aun siendo justificable y útil tener en cuenta las teorías de la mente cuando se consideran aspectos de salud mental y psicoterapia, es también deseable tomar en consideración las estructuras de la sociedad responsables por generar las condiciones de bienestar o malestar, además de que es también importante reflexionar acerca de cómo podrían cambiarse estas condiciones. Según Rustin, la contra-cultura y de alguna manera el modelo post-modernista que informa el symposium, solamente pueden formar parte de una respuesta lo suficientemente adecuada a los problemas identificados en el symposium.

In queste note, Michael Rustin rilegge i contributi del simposio, delineandone i principali obiettivi e argomentazioni. Egli prosegue offrendo alcune riflessioni critiche e ponendo interrogativi relativi al concetto chiave di 'stato terapeutico'. Egli osserva come poca attenzione sia data alle teorie psicoanalitiche o ad altre teorie psicologiche della mente come distinte dai modelli biologici, principale oggetto di critica nel simposio. Egli sostiene che sia giustificato e utile tenere in considerazione le teorie della mente nel valutare le questioni relative alla salute e alla terapia della mente, per questo è opportuno analizzare anche le strutture sociali, che hanno la responsabilità di generare condizioni di benessere o malessere mentale, così da poter anche riflettere su come sia possibile modificarle. Il paper sostiene che l'approccio critico 'post-moderno' e contro-culturale che caratterizza il simposio può costituire solo una parte di un'adeguata risposta ai problemi che il simposio identifica.

Dans son commentaire, Michael Rustin passe en revue les articles du congrès, soulignant leurs principaux objectifs et arguments. Il offre ensuite des réflexions critiques posant des questions quant au concept-clé d' 'Etat thérapeutique'. Il remarque que la différence entre les théories de l'esprit psychanalytiques ou psychologiques et les modèles biologiques, principale critique de ce congrès, est peu explorée. Il propose que tout comme il est justifiable et utile de prendre en compte les théories de l'esprit lorsqu'on considère les problèmes de santé mentale et la thérapie, il est également souhaitable de tenir compte des structures de la société responsables de l'émergence des conditions de bien ou de mal-être et de réfléchir sur ce qui peut être modifié. Ce commentaire soutient que l'approche critique contre-culturelle et quelque part 'post-moderne' qui sous-tend ce congrès ne peut fournir qu'une réponse partielle aux problèmes identifiés dans ce congrès.

Σε αυτό το σχόλιο, ο Michael Rustin εξετάζει τα άρθρα στο συμπόσιο, περιγράφοντας τους κύριους στόχους και τα επιχειρήματά τους. Στη συνέχεια παρέχει κάποιους κρίσιμους αναστοχασμούς, με ερωτήσεις σχετικά με τη βασική έννοια της «θεραπευτικής στάσης». Ο ίδιος σημειώνει ότι έχει δοθεί λίγη προσοχή στην ψυχαναλυτική ή άλλες ψυχολογικές θεωρίες του νου που διακρίνονται από τα βιολογικά μοντέλα, τα οποία αποτελούν το κύριο αντικείμενο της κριτικής στο συμπόσιο. Ισχυρίζεται ότι, όπως ακριβώς είναι δικαιολογημένο και χρήσιμο να ληφθούν υπόψη οι θεωρίες του νου για τη μελέτη των θεμάτων της ψυχικής υγείας και της θεραπείας, έτσι είναι σκόπιμο να ληφθούν υπόψη και οι δομές της κοινωνίας που έχουν την ευθύνη για τη δημιουργία συνθηκών ψυχικής υγείας ή ασθένειας, και να προβληματιστούν σχετικά με το πώς αυτές μπορούν να αλλάξουν. Ο σχολιασμός υποστηρίζει ότι η αντι-πολιτισμική και κάπως «μεταμοντέρνα», κριτική προσέγγιση η οποία προβάλλει στο συμπόσιο μπορεί να αποτελεί μέρος μόνο μιας επαρκούς, κατάλληλης απάντησης στα προβλήματα που εντοπίζει το συμπόσιο.

The aim of this symposium of articles is to develop a critique of the dominant psychiatric paradigm which now defines mental illness, and to outline alternative psychotherapeutic approaches to mental suffering. It presents papers originally given at an international conference, held in Norway in 2014, with strong but not exclusively Scandinavian representation, which brought together practitioners and researchers committed to social constructionist approach to mental distress, that is to say one which is relational and anti-authoritarian. 'Beyond the therapeutic state' was the conference's title. The symposium is a coherent and persuasive advocacy of a position of 'critical psychotherapy'. This article reviews its main arguments, and in its second part offers some partially divergent reflections on how issues of mental health discussed in the symposium should be responded to.

An outstanding paper in my view is the first, 'Children's mental health: Time to stop using psychiatric diagnosis', by Sami Timimi. This develops a well-sourced critical analysis of the 'medical model' of illness and treatment as this is applied in what it calls hegemonic psychiatric practice to mental health, in particular to that of children, although most of its arguments apply to adult services as well. Its thesis can be stated in the following way. In the field of physical illness and treatment, there is no doubt that the 'medical model' has been and indeed remains a successful one. Its science is based on fundamental discoveries about the body and its processes, and continues to advance in its scope. We can add to the author's summary that it is often able to connect symptoms (pains, losses of function, weakness) to their causes, in identifiable diseases or organic malfunctions, sometimes with definite causal agents – bacterial or viral infections, fractures, tumours, immune deficiencies, etc. It has developed batteries of 'technologies' – medical interventions – which have been able to respond to both symptoms and their causes. Entire diseases (e.g. smallpox, polio) have been eradicated through immunization, or if they haven't yet been it is only because their known remedies have not yet been comprehensively applied. The course of many illnesses can be fairly accurately anticipated, once diagnoses have been made, with predictable success rates for specified treatments.

There are of course many criticisms that can be made of this 'medical model' even as it has been applied to physical health. Medicine is sometimes omnipotently attached to the idea of cure, at the expense of sparing patients avoidable suffering. There is often insufficient regard paid to psycho-social and relational issues bearing on illness and recovery. There are many distortions in expenditure priorities, for example where investment in research on diseases and their remedies does and does not take place. Environmental and social causes play a large part in the differential incidence of illness – life expectancy differs between social classes in the UK by as much as 10 years. But for all the qualifications one can make, the author of this paper is clear that physical medicine, essentially, works.

Quite the opposite is the case, he argues, for the sphere of psychiatry and mental illness. In this field, there is no level of explanation for most 'illnesses' at a more profound level than that of their symptoms. The diagnostic categories used in psychiatry are essentially descriptors, supported by no basic scientific discoveries about the nature or causes of mental illness. 'Unlike the rest of medicine', he writes, 'which has developed diagnostic systems that build on an aetiological and pathophysiological framework, psychiatric diagnostic manuals such as DSM 5 and ICD-10 have failed to connect diagnostic categories with aetiological processes. Thus, there are no physical tests referred to in either manual that can be used to help establish a diagnosis'. The diagnostic categories systemized in the two major diagnostic manuals are little more than changing catalogues of symptoms, to which are often attached pharmacological interventions whose only claim to effectiveness is in symptom reduction. 'None of our medications treat a biological abnormality and none have been shown to improve long-term outcomes'.

In physical medicine, the discovery of remedies has often led to the reduction in the incidence and severity of illnesses. But in psychiatry, especially child psychiatry which is this paper's main subject, the writer points out that the reverse has in fact been the case. The coincident rise in classified illnesses and medications deemed to treat them suggests both that the availability (and marketability) of the medications has been driving the diagnostic system, and also that the persistence of some conditions (such as depression) may for many sufferers even be the outcome of long-term dependence on medications. In a telling analysis, the writer points out that some of the NICE recommendations for pharmacological treatments are virtually unsupported by the evidence which NICE cites to justify them.

Like most other papers in this collection, this paper holds that mental illnesses are constructed by means of social and cultural definition. It suggests that there is a 'colonial' model at work, in which western definitions of mental illness are being propagated across the world in part in order to increase the marketing opportunities for the pharmaceutical industry.

The author Sami Timimi has set out a compelling critique, which deserves to be widely read among mental health practitioners. If he is right, the reality is that mental health requires a quite different form of understanding, and therefore also quite different forms of preventative and remedial intervention, than physical illness. It is to be noted that the author is not anti-rationalist, anti-scientific or anti-technological in general principle, as some contributors to this symposium appear implicitly to be. His interest is in showing where such forms of scientism are actually applicable, and where by contrast they have (so far) failed.

Other papers in the collection complement Timimi's critique. 'The Triumph of American Psychiatry: How It Created the Modern Therapeutic State' by Robert Whitaker describes the development of the psychiatric hospital and psychiatry profession. It chooses as its starting point the earlier humane origin of the asylum in the Quaker institution of the 'retreat' first set up in 1796, in which people with mental difficulties could be given seclusion, time and sympathetic care in which they could recover. This model was later, however, appropriated and radically transformed by the emerging medical sub-profession of psychiatry, with the invention of the custodial mental hospital, as a major institution of the therapeutic state. In the later nineteenth century and early twentieth century, eugenics had a role in this take-over, with its idea that mental illness had a genetic basis, and could contaminate society unless its sufferers were segregated. In the mid-twentieth century growing public hostility to incarceration and harsh treatment in mental hospitals[1] gave opportunity to psychoanalysts to gain influence for 'the couch' as a preferred therapy, at one point giving them a degree of hegemony in American psychiatry. But then the psychoanalysts (never very influential in British psychiatry) were displaced by another version of 'care in the community', with the emergence of new psychotropic medications as the supposed cure for mental illnesses. Drugs were marketed vigorously, for example as remedies which it was claimed would work 'as well as insulin did for diabetes'. The outcome has been a situation in which there has been a proliferation of psychiatric diagnoses, few with scientific merit, and of dependence on medication, with 20% taking drugs on a daily basis. The author proposes a return to the 'moral therapy' of the Quakers, though without consideration of how far this might depend on the larger context of Quaker beliefs and practices.

John Shotter, in his chapter, 'Psychiatric diagnoses, "thought styles", and *ex post facto* fact fallacies' provides a critique of the philosophical assumptions which he holds underpins modern beliefs about mental illness and its treatments. The argument is based on a critique of the rationalistic Cartesian assumptions of psychological science. It holds that linear causal reasoning, and the idea that the mind consists of nameable entities capable of being identified and manipulated, as it were 'from outside', is false. 'Living in two-way, *dialogical* relations with our surroundings, rather than in monological, one-way causal relations with them', the writer states, 'means that we can no longer treat ourselves as inquiring simply into a world of "things" already existing in the world around us. We need to see ourselves instead as always acting "from within" a still-in-process world of flowing streams of intermingling activities affecting us as much, if not more, than we can affect them. In such a world as this, instead of discovering pre-existing things in our inquiries, we continually bring such "things" into existence'. What this practically amounts to is the need to create a context of dialogue with persons suffering from mental distress, in which they can find meaning in their experience, and develop more tenable ways of being with themselves and others. Examples are given of individuals who have indeed been helped by such experiences, which are persuasive as such particular instances can often be.

The two subsequent chapters in the collection, 'Stories from the extended therapy room', and 'From victimhood to sisterhood- A practice based reflexive inquiry in to narrative informed group work with women who have experienced sexual abuse' each provide examples of how therapies can be conducted which are in sympathy with the philosophical approaches of the symposium. The first of these, by Carina Håkansson, is based on work over 25 years within the Family Care Foundation, founded in 1987.[2] It seems that this project was developed to provide an alternative to both psychiatric and psychoanalytic approaches to mental illness; it is rather clearer from the chapter what its own approach to mental disturbance is not, than how its practice is actually designed, although a kind of fostering in family settings is described as one exemplary practice. The writer describes the necessity to be deeply open to the experience of the persons whom the 'extended therapy room' is intended to help, and for the need for this to be a work of co-operation between therapists with one another, and with their clients, in which boundaries and distinctions between them remain fluid, unlike in models of practice which assign expertise to some and ignorance to others. The writer refers to making sense of her years of work on her thesis, and one has the sense that this paper may represent its consolidation in a scholarly form. The chapter gives one confidence in the integrity and deep commitment of the work which is described.

The chapter on narrative work with women who have come together in response to experiences of sexual abuse is primarily concerned to outline and justify a method of work which is both a form of practice and of research. The central idea, much influenced by feminist thought and practice, is that the sharing of painful experiences in a group can be a way of achieving recovery and growth. In a way which avoids the stigmatization and pathologization of therapeutic practices which identify sufferers as mere victims, rather than as subjects capable of reflecting on their own experiences in a relationship with others. The article was written at an early stage in the writer's doctoral project, when little of her fieldwork had been undertaken. There will be more to be learned when the outcome of this practice/research can be described.

The final chapter of the symposium, 'Radical Presence: Alternatives to the Therapeutic State' returns to the theoretical argument of the symposium. It develops a Foucauldian argument, drawing also on the writing of Nikolas Rose, against the systems of the human sciences or 'discourses', and their controlling effects in modern life. This is 'because no matter what professional domain we encounter, we offer ourselves to the surveillance of experts – expert doctors, expert scholars, expert therapists, expert politicians, expert managers'. These amount to a regulated 'therapeutic state' or 'psy-complex'. The aim of the chapter is to 'envision alternatives to popularized, dominant, individualizing, and frequently pathologizing forms of life … and to explore and imagine alternatives to individualized pathology'. The positive argument is for a relational concept of well-being, and for the development of forms of practice which can help to bring this about. The 'psy-complex' of rationalizing psychological discourses is assigned the major causal responsibility for bringing about these prevailing individualist mentalities. The author acknowledges that his argument might seem rather vague in its implications for practice, and offers examples to give it specific definition. One example is the Family Care Foundation, previously discussed, whose ethos and ways of working it explains. A second, in an unlikely re-appropriation of behavioural psychologists' interest in rats, describes a project in which isolated rats were freed from addiction to morphine through being returned to their normal social relationships with others of their species. The third describes a community survey in New York City of public attitudes to biological approaches to mental illness. This found strong antipathy to diagnosis and medicalization, and a preference which was based on 'talking to people – therapy, counselling, group therapy being the most common', together with social activities and life style changes 'volunteering, hobbies, music, dance, writing, meditation, exercise, yoga, diet, prayer and creating community'.

A great deal of weight is placed in this article, and in the whole collection, on adopting a committed, relational approach to mental suffering, and the papers communicate the spirit of this convincingly, in their different ways. The author of the final paper is advocating the development of a 'radical presence', while being careful not to entirely dismiss the whole formal system of mental health care. This idea of creating a 'presence' to exist alongside a 'psy-complex' and a 'therapeutic state' seems however a modest goal, considering how strongly the 'psy-complex' and 'therapeutic state' are being criticized in the symposium.

## Commentary

Interesting and broadly consistent with one another in spirit as these papers are, they bring to mind some critical questions. One of these concerns the analysis of the 'therapeutic state' and 'psy-complex' which underpins much of the argument of the symposium. While the idea of the 'therapeutic state' might seem to assign a great deal of causal responsibility to governments, the arguments of the papers do not support that analysis. In the paper on the development of American psychiatry, the principal agents in the regressive process described are the 'guild' or profession of psychiatry – at one time dominated in the USA by psychoanalysis – and the corporate manufacturers and distributors of drugs. But neither professions nor corporations are mere instruments of the state – indeed psychoanalysis has for most of its history existed in a space distinct from government, and in many societies has been viewed with great suspicion by it. States are best understood as functioning as the mediators and agents of forces, whose social and economic basis lies outside themselves. Imagine for example that the NHS in Britain became largely privatized (now a far from unlikely prospect), and that health care was based, as in the USA, on private medical insurance, albeit of a state-regulated kind. Does anyone imagine that the contraction of the role of the state in such a system would reduce the power of the medical model, or of the pharmaceutical companies, or of the medical profession? The United States experience strongly suggests the exact opposite.

The symposium takes as its starting point, in its opening chapter, the rejection of biological and medicalizing models of mental illness, and goes on to recommend broadly 'relational' and ethically focused alternatives to this. What is however absent is a serious consideration of substantial theorizations of the mind and its functions which are not primarily biological or 'medicalised', such as those of attachment theory and psychoanalysis.[3] Although Freud began his work as a neurologist, and was always interested in the biological substrata of the mind, essentially psychoanalysis, and its part-relative attachment theory, are theories of the mind and its functions, not of the body or the brain, and have become increasingly so as they have developed. Core psychoanalytic concepts such as unconscious mental function, anxiety, repression, splitting, transference, counter-transference and containment, have proved highly serviceable in understanding what can go wrong in mental life, both during infant and child development and during adult life. Furthermore, they have proved capable of significant development, and of expansion in their scope of explanation. The discovery of the possibility of child analysis by Melanie Klein and her colleagues is one such instance, the elaboration of attachment theory through more conventional experimental methods is another. Indeed, one rather suspects that many psychotherapists who disavow any particular commitment to the theories the theories of psychoanalysis, in practice find themselves making everyday use of many of its central concepts to make sense of their work with patients.

The contributors to this symposium in effect repudiate the idea that there is any systematic or cumulative body of knowledge of the mind, or of therapeutic techniques, for working with its dysfunctions, which can or should guide therapeutic work. Particularity, complexity and an ethical approach, they imply, is all, without need for theoretical framings. Implicit is a post-modern repudiation of the idea of 'truth' or 'objectivity', a social constructivist emphasis on 'difference' being preferred. (The significant place of Foucauldian perspectives in the symposium marks out its post-modern affinities.) One might say that guiding principles are being looked for in the discourses of philosophy and ethics, rather than those of the sciences, of any variety. Perhaps consistent with this, references to psychoanalysis are few, and those there are regrettably slighting and superficial. However, it does not seem possible to seriously argue that the psychoanalysts' and attachment theorists' attention to early development as a cause of later disturbance has been misplaced, even though it is far from simple to decide how such developmental issues should be engaged therapeutically.

There is better evidence than the first paper allows for the efficacy of the interventions derived from these 'mentalistic' perspectives. The capacity of attachment models to explain and indeed predict patterns of development, including across generations, has been amply demonstrated. The literature on the outcomes of psychoanalytic psychotherapy with children and adolescents (Kennedy, Kennedy, 2004; Kennedy & Midgley, 2007; Trowell, 2012) also indicates, that these methods achieve considerably better outcomes than routine psychiatric treatments.[4] The fact that these results can be achieved by practitioners from different therapeutic schools does not invalidate their theories, since therapists from different schools of psychoanalysis share many fundamental assumptions. Is it to be doubted that those who have been more deeply trained in psychotherapetic methods, and have learned something substantial about their own 'internal world' in the process, are likely to achieve better results as therapists than practitioners who bring only good intentions to their work?

There are two dimensions of what one might call 'structure' or 'causality' which this symposium has largely avoided. One of these concerns the explanation of mental distress and disturbance in terms of structures of the mind, such as have been evolved by psychoanalysis and by attachment theory with its concept of 'internal working models.' The other is the understanding of the social structures which give rise to the individualized, pathologizing and regulatory mentalities to which the contributors are rightly antipathetic. The implicit argument of the collection is that it is the 'psy-complex' – that is its ideologies and discourses – which is determinant, and that it is just a matter of human choice to repudiate these discourses and to think and act in different ways. But doesn't it seem likely that significant causal powers also lie elsewhere, in the larger social and economic systems of which the 'psy-complex' is one agent, albeit a significant one. The anxieties of children in schools, students in colleges, individuals dependent on long-term medication to keep going, the scapegoating of minorities and migrants, the depression caused by unemployment and insecurity, the pointless and destructive imprisonment of many deprived and depressed people, are malfunctions of a social system, not merely manifestations of a psy-complex or a 'therapeutic state'. One needs to develop alternatives to these structures and systems which create stress and disadvantage.

It seems in some ways to be a mis-characterization of our present state to describe it as a therapeutic state at all. (One remembers John Major's call for us to 'understand a little less'.) Indeed, those committed to a relational view of society (Rustin, 2014) might wish for the state to become more and not less therapeutic than it has now become. Where are the resources and commitments to come from to provide the more sympathetic, non-stigmatizing and non-judgemental care that those suffering from psychosocial problems are rightly thought by the contributors to need? Are the substantial professions of teachers, nurses, doctors, social workers, and indeed psychologists and psychotherapists, who generally have more sympathetic approaches to these issues than those in many other occupations, to be simply excluded from the idea of care, because they work for, or are regulated by, the 'therapeutic state'? Are the struggles in which many who work in these fields are engaged to defend human-responsive forms of care, against worsening kinds of instrumental and short-termist pressures, to be dismissed? What theory of social and political agency do the editors and authors of this symposium have in mind, when they call for alternatives to psychiatric models? Isn't it necessary for those involved in this work to see themselves not as against the state (thus against the role of government as such), but rather as working, as a radical group of social scientists once put it, 'both in and against the state'? (London Edinburgh Return Group, London Edinburgh Weekend Return Group, 1980). That is, to defend, in the agencies of government as well as in other settings, approaches which are respectful of people and their needs, and which do not adopt irrelevant and often harmful kinds of medicalized remedies for psychosocial conditions.

Psychotherapies of the counter-culture, and a 'radical presence', are not, by themselves, enough, to respond to the situation which this symposium identifies, which is one of great pain and distress, however the 'psy-complex' may choose to label it.

## Notes

1. The 'decarceration' movement led by Basaglia and other radicals in Italy was exemplary. (Foot, 2015). In the United States, Erving Goffman 's writing was influential in this development, and in Britain in the 1960s, R.D. Laing's.
2. The Family Care Foundation is further discussed in the final paper.
3. One could add the unmentioned cognitive behaviour therapy to this list, since it is 'mentalistic' and not biological in its basis, and of course has also been argued for forcefully in the *Improved Access to Psychological Therapies* programme, in opposition to medication, whatever view one may take of its actual evidence-base and of its antipathy to dynamic psychotherapies.
4. It is not generally feasible to assess the value of psychotherapies through randomized controlled trials, as it has been many physical medicines, because of the many variabilities that are involved. But this is not to say that on an exemplary basis, this should not be done from time to time, as it has been.

## References

Foot, J. (2015). *The man who closed the asylums: Franco Basaglia and the revolution in mental health care*. London: Verso.

Kennedy, E.(2004) *Child and adolescent psychotherapy: A systemic review of approaches*. London: North Central London Strategic Health Authority. Retrieved from http://www.efpp.org/research/systematic_review.pdf

Kennedy, E., & Midgley, N. (2007). *Process and outcome research in child, adolescent and parent–infant psychotherapy: A thematic review*. London: North Central London Strategic Health Authority. Retrieved from http://www.efpp.org/research/Process%20and%20Outcome.pdf

London Edinburgh Weekend Return Group. (1980). *In and against the state*. London: Pluto Press.

Rustin, M. J. (2014). A relational society. In S. Hall, D. Massey, & M. Rustin (Eds.), *After neoliberalism: The Kilburn manifesto*. London: Lawrence and Wishart. Retrieved from http://www.lwbooks.co.uk/journals/soundings/pdfs/Soundings%20Manifesto_Rustin.pdf

Trowell, J. (Ed.). (2012). *Childhood depression: A place for psychotherapy*. London: Karnac.

# Dark clouds

Chris Oakley

This essay is in part a response to a cluster of papers from the conference in Norway. Utilising these as a springboard to expand certain ideas, some latent, some more manifest in the papers, regarding the history and the terrain concerning the mental health issues in our culture. Fundamentally, this proposes that there is an unrelenting tension between two polarities: one reactionary and authoritarian, fixated on a concern with outcomes, propped up by closed systems of thought, managerial, habitually linked to adaptation and conformity; the other more romantically seen as revolutionary, unhandcuffing madness from mental illness, facilitating more expansive, freewheeling possibilities within all our lives. Much of this pays tribute to some of the major figures in the history of 'anti-psychiatry' (Basaglia, Cooper and Laing), with the costs involved, and goes on to trace out the genesis and consequences of the two predominant 'clouds' permeating our world, the paranoid and the digital … all converging on a naturalisation of our culture of surveillance, and an insistence on control. Otherwise known as a culture of fear.

Dieser Essay ist teilweise eine Erwiderung auf einige Artikel der Konferenz in Norwegen. Ausgehend von diesen sollen, mehr oder weniger latente bzw. manifeste, Ideen in den Artikeln mit Blick auf Geschichte und 'Terrain' psychischer Gesundheitsthemen in unserer Kultur weiterverfolgt und -entwickelt werden. Im Grunde ist damit eine dauerhafte Spannung zwischen zwei Polen intendiert: eine reaktionäre und autoritäre, fixiert auf Sorgen um Ergebnisse. Unterstützt von geschlossenen Gedankensystemen, managerhaftes Verhalten, habituell verbunden zu Adaption und Konformität. Die andere, mehr romantische, revolutionär verstandene, ungezügeltem Wahnsinn durch psychische Krankheiten, welches weitreichendere und lockere Möglichkeiten für alle von uns ermöglicht. Vieles davon zollt einigen der Hauptfiguren in der Geschichte der 'Anti-Psychiatrie' Anerkennung (Basaglia, Cooper and Laing) – den Folgen inklusive. Es führt uns weiter zur Entstehung und den gegenwärtig sich abzeichnenden Konsequenzen zweier "Schatten", die unsere Welt durchdringen – der Paranoidität und dem Digitalen. Alles kulminiert in einer Naturalisierung unserer Kultur hinsichtlich Überwachung und dem Beharren auf Kontrolle. Besser bekannt als Kultur der Angst.

Este artículo es en parte una respuesta a un conjunto de ponencias presentadas en una conferencia en Noruega, utilizándolos como trampolín para expandir ciertas ideas, algunas latentes, otras expresadas en ellos, en relación con la historia y los aspectos concernientes a la salud mental en nuestra cultura. Básicamente se ha propuesto que existe una tensión constante entre dos polaridades: una reaccionaria y autoritaria sólamente preocupada en obtener resultados, apoyada en esquemas de pensamiento rígidos, gerencial, habitualmente asociada con adaptación y conformidad; otra, románticamente vista como como revolucionaria, que trata de liberar los problemas de salud mental de los rótulos impuestos por la sociedad y que facilita una mayor expansión y liberación de las posibilidades en nuestras vidas. Gran parte de esta posición reconoce el valor del trabajo de grandes figuras de la ''anti-psiquiatría'' (Basaglia, Cooper, Laing) con su implícito costo, y sigue el rastro del origen y las consecuencias de las dos ''nubes '' que ensombrecen nuestro mundo: la paranoide y la digital, y que convergen en una naturalización de nuestra cultura de vigilancia y en la insistencia en el control, de otra manera, la conocida como la cultura del miedo.

Questo contributo è, in parte, risposta ad un insieme di interventi della conferenza tenutasi in Norvegia. Essi sono utilizzati come "trampolino di lancio' per ampliare idee, alcune latenti, altre più esplicite, pertinenti ciò che attiene l'ambito e la storia dei problemi di salute mentale nella nostra cultura. Fondamentalmente si avanza l'idea che ci sia una tensione incessante tra due polarità: una reazionaria e autoritaria, bloccata alla preoccupazione degli esiti, sostenuta da sistemi di pensiero chiusi, manageriali, normalmente fermi all'adattamento e alla conformità; l'altra più romanticamente vista come rivoluzionaria, che 'toglie le manette' alla follia imprigionata dalla malattia mentale, consentendo maggior ampiezza e libertà alle nostre esperienze di vita. Molto di ciò rende omaggio ad alcune delle figure più importanti nella storia dell'antipsichiatria (Basaglia, Cooper e Laing), con i 'costi' da essa implicati, e prosegue tracciando la genesi e le conseguenze delle due 'nuvole' predominanti che permeano il nostro mondo, il paranoico e il digitale ... tutti concordi sulla naturalizzazione dell'attuale cultura alla sorveglianza e sull'insistenza sul controllo. Altrimenti nota come una cultura della paura.

Cet article est en partie une réponse à une série d'articles issus d'une conférence en Norvège. Ils sont utilisés comme tremplin pour développer des idées, certaines latentes, d'autres plus manifestes exprimées dans ces articles concernant l'histoire et le champ des problèmes de santé mentale dans notre culture. Il est avancé qu'il existe une tension fondamentale et incessante entre deux polarités : l'une réactionnaire et autoritaire obnubilée par les résultats, sous tendue par des systèmes de pensée fermés, managériaux, généralement liés à l'adaptation et à la conformité ; et l'autre considérée de manière plus romantique comme révolutionnaire, déliant la folie de la santé mentale, offrant des possibilités plus grandes, pour mener nos vies en roue libre en quelque sorte. Beaucoup de ceci rend hommage à quelques une des figures majeures de l'histoire de l'anti psychiatrie (Basaglia, Cooper et Laing) avec ce que cela implique et retrace la genèse et les conséquences des deux nuages qui assombrissent notre monde: le paranoïde et le digital... Les deux convergeant vers une banalisation de notre culture de la surveillance et de l'insistance du contrôle, autrement connue comme culture de la peur.

Το παρόν άρθρο αποτελεί εν μέρει απάντηση σε μια σειρά δημοσιεύσεων από το συνέδριο στη Νορβηγία. Χρησιμοποιεί αυτές ως εφαλτήριο για την επέκταση ορισμένων ιδεών στα άρθρα, κάποιες άδηλες, κάποιες περισσότερο έκδηλες, σχετικά με την ιστορία και το πεδίο της ψυχικής υγείας στον πολιτισμό μας. Βασικά στο παρόν άρθρο προτείνεται ότι το πεδίο χαρακτηρίζεται από μια συνεχή ένταση ανάμεσα σε δύο πόλους: έναν αντιδραστικό και αυταρχικό, προσαρμοσμένο σε μια ενασχόληση με τα αποτελέσματα, που στηρίζεται σε κλειστά συστήματα σκέψης, λειτουργεί διαχειριστικά και συνήθως συνδέεται με την προσαρμογή και τη συμμόρφωση. Ο άλλος πόλος θεωρείται πιο ρομαντικός και επαναστατικός, ότι απελευθερώνει την τρέλα από τις ψυχικές ασθένειες και ότι διευκολύνει την ανάπτυξη των δυνατοτήτων στη ζωή όλων μας. Για πολλά από αυτά οφείλουμε φόρο τιμής σε κάποιες από τις σημαντικότερες προσωπικότητες στην ιστορία της «αντι-ψυχιατρικής» (Basaglia, Cooper και Laing), με όλο το κόστος που εμπεριέχεται, και συνεχίζεται ο δρόμος προς τη γένεση και τις συνέπειες των δύο κυρίαρχων «σύννεφων» που επισκιάζουν τον κόσμο μας, το παρανοϊκό και το ψηφιακό ... όλα συγκλίνουν στην αποδοχή, στον πολιτισμό της επιτήρησης και της επιμονής για έλεγχο. Διαφορετικά γνωστή ως μια κουλτούρα φόβου.

It was ever thus. Allowing for an oversimplification, a narrow mindedness even, what frames the kaleidoscopic cullings from the collection of papers from the conference in Norway, all in their separate ways attempting to address prevailing concerns about the 'Therapeutic State', are the habitual conflicting poles of, to utilise psychiatric terminology, the stultifications of the paranoid and the wilfulness of attention-deficit disorders. For some of us, the world may be divided into those of us who are paranoid and those of us who are too paranoid to be paranoid. Paranoia no longer taken to be the colloquially understood debilitating sense that everyone is out to get you, but rather an insistent investment in the imagined possibility of a rendezvous with an ultimate truth. In other words a last word, we have got it all down, a totalisation of the multiplicities of our ways of being in this world, all culminating in a manageable and ultimately closed system. All generating 'universally applicable categories', characteristically concerned with statistical accumulation to prop up a project of conformist adaptation. As one of the writers pointed out, so much of this is underpinned by the foundational assumption as to what is taken to be normal. And this has an unvarying tilt in the direction of being obedient, to behave in ways that are not disturbing, 'disturbed' so often merely being a designation of somebody who is 'disturbing'. Again, so often, to the ones who are in power.

In opposition to such concerns are another camp entirely. There we find a valorisation of something quite other: a desire to pay no attention to concern with outcomes, always the hallmark of the former. As if there is a wanton disregard for such considerations, and for so many this invites the criticism of an irresponsibility, a disorder, a deficit with regard to the very order that the former seek to impose. A romantic simplification suggests one is on the side of the reactionary, fascistic even, the other more on the side of the revolutionary, the freewheeling.

But could it ever be so simple. Perhaps to a degree we are all subordinated to this conflict, all ensnared by its web. In all probability an impossible undertaking to do other than inhabit the tension, present in all therapies, between art and science, between the warmth of individuality and the cooler vigour of generalisable principles. To accept the hypocrisies and inadequacies of contemporary psychiatry and the therapies, to endure without complaint unquestionably gives rise to a certain suffering, the despair of not being in despair to follow Kierkegaard. But to spend a life in permanent dissent may exact a higher price. The examples of Lang and Cooper come to mind. One of the curiosities of the papers stemming from the conference is what, at least in some quarters, would appear to be a form of disregard and yet simultaneously such a claim runs the risk of being indelibly London-centric. Almost as if the Roundhouse in Chalk Farm, the site of The Dialectics of Liberation conference in 1967, was the one and only centre of a particular set of initiatives, which clearly in a variety of forms continue to this day, with the names of the British 'anti-psychiatrists', Lang, Cooper and Maxwell Jones so very much to the fore. Nevertheless at that time, their time, they were indeed in the vanguard of so many of the concerns of the more recent conference in Norway. All seeking to disrupt, to disperse psychiatric discourses with its unrelenting tendency to read off the so-called mentally ill as less than, to define, to enslave, to pathologise and to constrain how we are together. Rather than demonise or medicalise purported mental illness they endeavoured to understand it's existential, social and political elements. The project was to allow the so-called 'patients' the potentially intoxicating but simultaneously somewhat dangerous freedom to explore, to experiment, to expand possibilities rather than to restrain and repress their crises. As Cooper (1978) said, the aim was to reveal whether the invalids were genuinely ill or had merely been invalidated.

Franco Basaglia is still something of a household name in Italy. And even the much discredited Laing was comparatively recently lionised in an editorial in the Guardian, one of the more distinguished British broadsheets. A particularly grotesque attempt to denigrate the hapless Laing was by the essayist Hitchens (2011) who, in a piece on the Baader Meinhof group, reduced his ideas to a seeking to 'persuade the pitifully insane that they needed no treatment save social revolution'. He went on to describe Laing's work as 'one of the major disorders of the 1960s.' (again, note the implicit emphasis on order). But back to Basaglia and what is known as 'his Law': Law 180, which effectively brought to an end the era of detention and repression of the 'mentally ill'. A culmination of a career spent on the psychiatric barricades. The Italian philosopher, Norberto Bobbio claimed that this was 'the only real reform' in Italian history. Basaglia during the 1960's held a position as director of a mental hospital in Gorizia, near the Yugoslav border. This was 15 years or so before Law 180 came into effect. During this time, both in Gorizia and later in Trieste his aim had been to install democracy within the asylum, moving in the direction of breaking down the hierarchical differentiation between staff and patients. Doctors, rather than being distinguished by their traditional white coats, now mixed more freely with the inmates as the good doctor went on refusing to sign the permits for any form of restraint. Locked wards were opened, bars, shackles and straightjackets removed. Inevitably (it was ever thus) he and his team, his 'equipe' of like-minded psychiatrists were faced with considerable opposition both from the old guard inside the hospitals and from the more conservative, paranoid elements from without. Despite his growing reputation, aided by the publication of 'L'Istituzione Negata' a collection of papers describing the radicalisation of the Gorizia regime which he edited, and a hugely flattering TV documentary, he never permitted himself any form of self-congratulation. He was only too well aware of the dangers lurking within the midst of the apparent emancipation.

At that time, the 1960s, I was doing as a part of my psychoanalytic apprenticeship a stint as a psychiatric social worker at Claybury Hospital, out in the East London suburbs of Woodford. Claybury had an interesting history. Despite in appearance, a typically Gothic 'insanity factory', and location, suitably outside 'the city walls', seeming entirely like a traditional mental hospital, it was actually a self-styled therapeutic community. There were 11 o'clock meetings held every day. Everybody involved was invited to come. Everybody included the administrative staff, the secretaries, the cleaners, even the groundsman who looked after the football pitch which was one of the first things that you would see as you swept up the drive. Unfortunately, the head honcho whose vision this was, Dr Martin, was now holed up in a pan-optic tower overlooking the cluster of buildings of which the hospital was comprised. Never appearing, having retreated, opting for the life of the recluse. As a social worker, I played a considerable part in facilitating the release of a man who, having spent a lengthy time in Broadmoor, the principal institution for the criminally insane in the UK, had now arrived at Claybury. Many years before, he had killed his wife. But he was now agitating to return home, where the tragedy had occurred, claiming that whatever treatments he had been subject to had done the trick. However, once reinstalled in his old house, it was only a matter of months before he had killed himself by battering his head against the living room wall. To this day, I continue to hesitate, am undecided as to whether it was the wrong thing to enable this discharge. I just don't know. For Basaglia, there were potentially even more distressing occurrences: in September 1968, a man released immediately returns home to kill his wife with a hammer. A few years later in February 1972, now at the hospital in Trieste, he authorised the release of somebody who later murdered both his parents. In other words, whatever we may come to understand about madness there truly are some genuinely crazy people in our midst, seriously dangerous both to others and to themselves. The price of replacing aloof pathologising with the solidarity of the Quakers and the 'brethren' (an early instance of the principle of allowing the 'illness' to run its course cited in one of the papers) may at times be extremely high. Which is not to suggest that it is not worth paying.

And the reason for mentioning some of the 'big' names from what is, after all, nigh on 50 years ago is that some of the papers under consideration appear to be almost wilfully ignorant of much of the history of such initiatives. To redress the balance as it were. No doubt it was of immense importance, after all these things need saying repeatedly, when at the end of the 1970s the Swedish therapist Barbro Sandin claimed that schizophrenia is not an illness but a reaction to something too hard to deal with. But it was hardly a novel idea. Laing and Esterson were saying something entirely along these lines in their book *Sanity, Madness and the Family* in 1964. And yet we can more than glimpse suffusing these contributions a sense of convergence, a sharing of particular sensibilities, a commitment to disrupt, to resist some of the more persistent tropes of contemporary psychiatry and indeed that of many of the current therapies. But here I seek to underline a vested interest. I am not merely a fan of psychoanalysis, although to co-opt something that Lacan said about Freud there is much that I could shit on, I earn a living from it. So perhaps it is not entirely surprising that it somewhat jars when Freud is momentarily reduced to merely being interested in making sense of the past. All marinated in the somewhat disparaging, mocking tone of 'Freud and his gospels'. Similarly, however inspirational something might be on a personal level, when reference to notions of 'commitment, openness and above all authenticity' inmixed with vigorous claims of 'creating a space where there is a chance of making sense of what is happening' along with 'being met as a real person by another real person' are all gathered together, recruited as it were, to suggest that such ideas have 'extended the knowledge and ideas about psychotherapy' the heart sinks. Pioneering? That's piffle. Such ideas are as old as the hills.

At certain moments, it feels as if there is considerable distress on two co-existing fronts. Regret that the 'Therapeutic State' (Szasz' term) appears to have colonised us all: either our suffering is increasingly suppressed as evidenced by the alarming rise of the percentage of people taking psychiatric medication or is corralled into a dubious faith in so-called experts from the plethora of the competing therapies on offer. And then, despite a critical recognition that a 'physics-laboratory approach to life' appears to be 'overwhelmingly influential' almost in the same breath, there is a bemoaning that psychiatry lacks 'the same scientific security of belonging to a technical model developed by research grounded in natural sciences … as is the rest of medicine.' Another writes of 'the not-easy-to-change socially shared background that we MUST change if we are ever going to conduct any truly SCIENTIFIC (my emphasis) inquiries into our actual nature'. It is moments such as these that I am reminded of the words of Jacques Lacan where he suggested that, in relation to psychoanalysis, those who placed their faith in science would be waiting a very long time for 'psychoanalysis is not a science … it is a delirium.' Quite.

So what are these prevailing tropes of the 'Psy or Therapeutic State'? So much appears to be frozen within the myth of interiority. In other words, there is something 'inside' either you or me that is the potential site for psychopathology. And this fantasy of an internal world does so much to uphold just such potentialities in this form of a basic assumption. Rather might we not acknowledge that we are all beings in the world, all subject to a myriad of societal pressures and discursive practices, otherwise known as the culture within which we dwell. In other words, we are only ever driven mad by others who in their turn have been, in their own way, been driven mad themselves. And as we touch on this subject whilst we may all have a variety of objectives, conscious and unconscious, do any of us actually have 'internal objects', all part of an alienating vocabulary that sustains the fiction. Indeed so much of the violence that lurks within the psychiatric field takes the form of the words used. One of the writers speaks of 'restraining definitions', a rather wonderful acknowledgement of precisely such difficulties, so exemplified by the emetic term 'service user'.

There appears to be considerable convergence, a collective desire to unshackle us all from any such manoeuvres, to move beyond the language of pathology and victimhood. The project being to disperse so many of the objectifying identities encoded in a whole variety of terms. Felix Guattari claimed 'never to have seen a schizophrenic' which some might find a little mystifying given that he was the head of the psychiatric hospital La Borde in the Loire Valley. But in a similar vein, I would claim to have never seen a psychoanalyst. All underwritten by the axiom 'whatever we take ourselves to be, we are not'. All this is heading towards a dismantling of diagnostic categories, of the dead hand of 'clinical structures' that continue to haunt so much of the psychiatric and psychoanalytical terrain. (I use the word psychoanalytic in the generic sense of covering the whole continuum of therapies, including counselling and case work). Indeed there is an immensely valuable contribution from the paper 'Psy discourses, "thought styles", and *ex post facto* fact fallacy' that points out that over and over again the following phenomena will occur: a set of attitudes and behaviour will be drawn together under a particular name, for example 'schizophrenia', and this will then be utilised, reified as a disease entity, inevitably lodged within, as that which gave rise to the set of attitudes and behaviour in the first place. And how crazy is that!

At times, we note a quite explicit aim to disrupt prevailing psychiatric discourse with its unceasing reliance on diagnosis, prognosis and the emphasis on outcomes. Outcomes almost invariably, but not inherently, concerned with returning the individual to a position of conformity. The back to work imperative, all obediently coerced into producing the endless supply of surplus so endemic to our neoliberal capitalist concerns. Entirely appropriately psychiatry is read off as a form of social control through defining, pathologising and constraining, all a form of policing the family. But perhaps it is a little too easy to engage in the self-congratulatory back slapping as we all agree in the virtue of dispersing concern with diagnosis and placing our bets on allowing an expansion of the multiplicities of ways of living a life. Brushing aside the dubious assertion that the 'psy-discourses' preceded the individualisation of our world, that such atomisation is a 'by-product of such a discourse' we can so easily collapse into a seriality of somewhat hollow assertions. In fairness, one of the authors somewhat wanly admits that she engages in a certain vagueness. But so often it feels as if we are terrain of the Yoko Ono's 'vote for peace' installations. Indeed we might all hold our hands up for that. Yet it is only and always just empty rhetoric. Similarly, the privileging of 'active attentiveness to processes of relating' might very well get everyone's vote but ultimately folds back on itself as the preferred mode of treatment, aka 'radical relating'. The claim is that there would be 'a very particular way of positioning ourselves in the world as opposed to creating formulas for correct or correcting action'. Unfortunately, it is difficult to avoid a sense that we are being invited to affirm a 'correct', not to mention 'correcting', way of going about things lurking in the midst of all. In other words, we have never genuinely moved beyond the confines of generalities, potentially to be upheld as true for all time, unwittingly crushing the potential for a singularity of approach.

As we move onto 'alternative forms of relating' or the 'radical presence of relational being' … audible sighs as pseud's corner beckons … all with an emphasis on 'living together', we come upon the curious claim to 'ultimately erase … the traditional boundaries of separation.' Allowing that the emphasis is intended to reside with 'traditional boundaries,' nevertheless there I was assuming that in order to be together we initially, traditionally even, had to be separate. And this is prior to the pomposity of a 'relational ethic'; whilst it is entirely laudable to eschew any search for standardised practice, any attempt to 'abandon reliance on abstract principles' congeals into the mire of notions such as 'difference and complexity' and 'interactive processes'. A little abstract in my book. All well and good to underline 'a curiosity for difference, openness … to form(ing) new understandings, a movement away from agreement or adjudication of perspectives' but ultimately it all smacks too much of good intentions and is ultimately as shallow as dear Yoko. With the strains of 'All you need is Love' pulsating in the back ground. Concerned that this is developing into notes for 'bad therapy awards' analogous to the 'bad sex awards' (an annual event in the UK for what is deemed to be the most excruciating attempts to describe an erotic moment), I want to stress that there will almost invariably be a peculiar tension. A tension between the importance, the directness of what is being said, always signifying an urgency, after all these are serious people doing their best in relation to serious issues, and the simultaneously crucial concern with the beauty, the sparkle of the saying. Perhaps we might all sign up for being identified with the 'wild freethinkers, unfettered by convention' but if it ain't got that swing it doesn't mean a thing. All this needs to be a song of life or risks being worth nothing at all. So many self-defining instances of superiority, so frequently verging on the moralistic that seep into ideas such as a 'relational ethic', where behind every therapist lurks a priest, have a tendency to lead to a potentially disastrous differentiation, a return to the spurious hierarchy of an 'us' and 'them'. All with the enhanced possibility of encouraging an identification with figures of authority. For, leaning heavily on Sartre, all ideologies are freedom whilst still in development, oppression once they are formed.

But for a moment let us return to the issue of paranoia. Potentially the incorrigible hallmark of our contemporary world. At a macrolevel, since the second half of the Twentieth century we have lived under the auspices of two clouds: the mushrooming terror cloud of the atomic bomb (see Jeff Nuttall's *Bomb Culture*, 1968) and more recently the proliferation of the cloud of information networks. Whist the mushroom cloud, an iconic symbol of post-war paranoia, represented the potential annihilation of our civilisation, only partly mitigated by the deterrence of the idea of Mutual Assured Destruction, the realities of digital space, the internet cloud represents a network driven, information saturated, set of conditions in which we increasingly live, work and play. These two interrelated clouds have infiltrated and embedded themselves into our everyday. The effects have colonised our world and are felt in our minds and bodies. Data overwhelm us with an oppressive force that the Jonathan Franzen, in his latest novel *Purity* (2015), has likened to Communist East Germany.

> You cannot not have a relation to, in the case of East Germany, the socialism of the State. In the case of the internet you can ignore it, or you can abet it. Either way you are in relation to it. And that is what is totalitarian. (Brockes, 2015)

Or to quote the Eagles and their 'Hotel California' 'You can check out any time you want, but you can never leave.'

The idea that there is an unstaunchable entanglement between these two clouds runs as follows. The familiar image of the mushroom cloud stems from the documentation of nuclear testings which began in 1945, followed by the horrendous bombing of Hiroshima and Nagasaki. And condensed in this representation of sublime terror and destructive potential was the wellspring for a specific need. Any potential command structure would have to have at its disposal an integrated system of distributed information networks, without which the deterrent possibilities would be nullified. Ultimately giving rise to what we now know as the internet. And advancing technologies have sufficiently evolved to allow us to access this in the palm of our hand. Digital and mobile equipment have now come to play such an inordinate role in our lives, and by the mid-2000s corporations such as Amazon began using the term 'cloud' to designate the architecture of this information. The cloud facilitates the increasing assumption and represents the possibility whereby the circulation of information will be able to resolve a multiplicity of complex problems or even manifest unconscious desires. We see, think and feel via the cloud. When this digitalised network emerged from the paranoia of the nuclear age, it simultaneously inaugurated a euphoric, utopian dimension in the form of a fantasised interconnected global community. We all live in the same village: itinerant Bedouins on their laptops watching 'Breaking Bad' in their tents in the desert. A political and social dream, or nightmare depending on perspective, from which arose global terrorism and online dating, presaging a deluge of self-disclosure. But this cloud has a mystifying dimension. It has a way of designating the vastness of available data and metaphor that masks, indeed clouds our perception, allowing a naturalisation of the networks of power and the expidential increase in surveillance that accompanies these so called advances. The German photographer, Horst Ademit coined the term 'cold rays' to point to the negative yet invisible forces that criss-cross unimpeded all the dimensions of our biological and psychological life, saturating our cultural and ecological systems. Despite a metaphor of immateriality, the shadow of this cloud imposes itself on the world as we have come to know it. Potentially, it transforms us into a thing, spoken for, ventriloquised by the prevailing capitalist insistences of commodification and consumption. The female body appropriated as merchandise, the model of the model, to facilitate the sale of more merchandise. A mere example.

The effects are inevitably multiple: from the corporal to the affective, from the political to the economic. A small illustration is that despite endless promises of increased leisure time this digital age has ushered in an era of increased average working hours. And to intensify the effects of the cloud, the big Other bearing down on us with its rallying call to 'enjoy!', we are caught up in a plurality of energy drinks (a recent beer advert proposes that 'living the dream means that one never sleeps' … the utopian fiction in which were we to relax we entertain the disastrous risk of missing out) all converging on the increased medicalisation of our lives. So should we really be so surprised that psychiatry and the therapies meekly comply in this regime of regimentation and surveillance. Whether it be drones, surveillance cameras, facial recognition software or biometric identification technologies, it all looks as if it is here to stay. As I write, my psychoanalytic organisation is about to be visited by a cluster of inspectors from the entirely wretched registering body, the UKCP, in order to audit our training. And we all meekly submit, quiescent in the face of a culture of managerialism. All enmeshed in a sullen resentment.

I think the problem with these papers is that none go far enough. A failure to cut to the core. No doubt there is an integrity to the initiatives with their calls for 'authenticity' and 'radical openness', and whilst there is a disappointment with the vapid and programmatic word-song drained of any real vigour, the concerns go further than that. It is as if no one genuinely steps outside the confines of diagnosis: now diagnosing the ills of psychiatry and psychotherapy and the proposed treatment? All converge on an emphasis on relationship. Although quite what this relationship might look like remains frustratingly obscure. The difficulty being that, and perhaps it is truly difficult for any of us to entirely escape this, all is still lodged in a system of belief, all still entangled in a false refuge, even if we allow that placing one's bets on science is rapidly coming in as a busted flush. Remember it was Foucault who initially saw psychoanalysis as on the side of regularisation, ultimately a violence, extruding singularity, all underwritten by a demand for adjustment, regimentation and repression. All aligned with the pan optic oppression. But later in his book *The Order of Things* (1970) he had changed his mind. Psychoanalysis was now on the side of the angels, behind the velvet rope of the privileged enclosure, the one place, in so many instances the only place, where the mad could find their voice, where they could speak.

So it feels utterly crucial to move in the following direction: whatever we take madness to be, for after all however slippery that term may be something of it does adhere, it seems utterly essential to cease to turn it into mental illness. Whenever this happens, it will automatically inaugurate a question of the preferred mode of treatment. With all that trails in its wake. The issue of competencies, of professionalism, of the nanny culture of 'mummy knows best'. Remember we are not treating anything. Let us begin from a place in which it is never assumed that there is something wrong with somebody, rather than on occasions something has gone wrong. Sometimes disastrously so. As Adam Phillips wrote (2010) 'we are all doing the best we can with what we've got'. Again it was Foucault who thought that there had to be a possibility that there would come a time when the entire concept of 'madness' would disappear. Not because it would be subsumed into the controlled space of mental illness ('great tepid aquariums') but because the limit designated by madness would be subordinated by a multiplicity of flows, all on the side of escaping control, eluding any overarching surveillance, all now co-joined by 'the serenity of the positive'. Of course these ideas of Foucault are only a mere potentiality, possibly wildly optimistic. Meanwhile, the paranoiac vector is already installed, is the actual, the actually realised prevailing system of authoritarian design. But what Foucault points us towards is a truly wonderful vision nevertheless.

## References

Brockes, E. (2015, August 21). Jonathan Franzen's interview: 'There is no way to make myself not male'. *The Guardian* [online]. Retrieved September 21, 2015, from http://www.theguardian.com/global/2015/aug/21/jonathan-franzen-purity-interview

Cooper, D. (1978). *The language of madness*. London: Allen Lane, Penguin.

Foucault, M. (1964). La Folie, l'absence d'œuvre [Madness, Absence of Œuvre]. *La Table Ronde, 196*, 11–21.

Foucault, M. (1970). *The order of things*. New York, NY: Pantheon Books.

Franzen, J. (2015). *Purity*. London: 4th Estate publishing.

Hitchens, C. (2011). *Arguably*. London: Atlantic Books.

Laing, R. D., & Esterson, A. (1964). *Sanity, madness and the family*. London: Tavistock.

Nuttall, J. (1968). *Bomb culture*. London: MacGibbon & Kee.

Phillips, A. (2010). *On balance*. London: Hamish Hamilton.

# Altermodernity and the unfortunate need to train critical psychotherapists and counsellors

Del Loewenthal

## Introduction

A brief history: The Critical Psychotherapy Network arose out of the conference 'Do We Need a Critical Psychotherapy? Exploring Talking Therapies in Neoliberal Society', held at the Freud Museum, London in June 2015. This in turn arose out of the book, Loewenthal, D. (2015) *Critical Psychotherapy, Psychoanalysis and Counselling: Implications for Practice*, which in turn arose out of my editorial, 'The unfortunate need for critical psychotherapy and counselling' (Loewenthal, 2013). I would like to speak briefly of the first item in this chain and then examine the thoughts that led up to it.

On our Critical Psychotherapy Network website (https://criticalpsychotherapy.wordpress.com/2015/06/27/critical-psychotherapy-manifesto/) we state:

> It is becoming increasingly difficult to find a place to speak freely. Psychotherapists, psychoanalysts and counsellors report that it is less and less possible to question organisational practice, fearful of overt or covert punishment. Academics in our universities fear for their jobs if they speak out. Most importantly, the therapeutic space itself has become subject to various insistences – what is sayable, what is hearable, what must be reported, what technique must look like. Neoliberalism, the rise in the audit culture, and the overregulation of therapy challenges such freedoms. So what do we do?

Further on this website in starting to answer this question we state:

> One of the Network's aims is to develop a manifesto for critical psychotherapy. We have traced out some ideas below building from the manifesto outlined in Critical Psychotherapy, Psychoanalysis and Counselling:

- We must resist threats to providing a therapeutic, confidential space. It is our ethical duty to challenge these threats, but we can only do this if we support one another.
- The training of talking therapists must include sociology, philosophy, anthropology, the arts and political economy. It must also develop trainees' skills to observe and deconstruct ideologies (including our own).
- We must not be seduced by methodologies that simply do not fit what we do. Instead we must find new ways of providing testimonial to ourselves, our colleagues and the public.

- We must be wary of state interventions and psychiatric nosology which threaten pluralism, and the clients' right to create a therapeutic space that works for them.
- We must be able to work with our own and others sexuality and violence.
- We need to recognise the cult of individualism can create suffering and overshadow the common good.
- We need to work actively around and outside the consulting room to inform and challenge public policy and discourse. Thinking about this must be part of future trainings.

I give the above (with grateful thanks also to our inaugural co-chair: Jay Watts) as an example of a way in which there are further developments (see also Brooker et al., 2017) that may be of use to others looking for ways to go beyond the increasing stranglehold of the therapeutic state. Below are what led to such developments, starting with a consideration of the underlying concerns that led to the 'unfortunate need for critical psychotherapy and counselling'.

To do this, the rest of this chapter is based on developments of three editorials (for the *European Journal of Psychotherapy & Counselling*). One of the editorials is about the unfortunate need for critical psychotherapy, which led me, as mentioned, to being asked to write *Critical Psychotherapy, Psychoanalysis and Counselling: Implications for Practice* (2015). I do consider that neoliberalism has now placed debilitating restrictions on psychotherapy, with one outcome being less and less possibility of providing a confidential space for clients to be able to speak about what is on their mind. In writing this, I am further convinced that something like a critical psychotherapy approach is vitally important for all therapies. (In my own case, one possibility is a critical existential-analytic approach [Loewenthal, 2020a], sometimes referred to as 'post-existential' [Loewenthal, 2011], and with which I am involved in critical psychotherapy therapy training through http://safpac.co.uk.)

The second editorial I have included provides both a dire warning of hypermodernity and the hope of altermodernity as a way out. I am amazed how, for example, the Campaign for Nuclear Disarmament is no longer a political force. I do not think this is because the risk of us blowing each other up has been significantly reduced, but more that the possibility is so imminent that we can no longer bear to think of it. The same is perhaps true with regard to our experience of alienation, where thoughtfulness is less possible both in our universities and our consulting rooms – far easier to take our minds off what is troubling us. This editorial it is hoped, when taken with the third editorial, 'Dracula, G8 and the training of critical psychotherapists and counsellors', provides a further argument for Carina Håkansson's chapter five: 'The extended therapy room'. If, as critical psychotherapists and counsellors, we can allow into our ways of working and living also the political, socio-economic factors this will hopefully enable us to become more alive not only for 'just you and me' but for all of us collectively. The chapter ends with some questions that might help bring about this different consciousness in training critical psychotherapists and counsellors.

## The unfortunate need for critical psychotherapy and counselling[1]

This editorial reluctantly put the case for the urgent need for 'critical psychotherapy and counselling' to have a permanent place in the syllabi of psychotherapy and counselling. This would be similar to psychology and psychiatry where niches are given to 'critical psychology' and 'critical psychiatry', tacitly implying that by and large psychology and psychiatry are examined uncritically.

Perhaps the main reason why this process has already taken place in psychology and psychiatry is that the prime role of these disciplines can be seen as agents of the state. At least in the UK, recent changes in government policy have greatly reduced any ability for those involved in counselling and psychotherapy to fundamentally question what they are doing. There has also been the long-standing argument that counselling and psychotherapy students receive trainings (mainly through private or charitable institutions), rather than an education, again uncritically putting forth their particular rivalrous gurus. Often this is done in such a way to make thoughtfulness a remote possibility – see for example, Kernberg's (1996) 'Thirty ways to destroy the creativity of psychoanalytic candidates'. Yet, for some, there was the hope, if indeed not the raison d'être, that universities might provide a space where society could allow the questioning of the assumptions underlying practices, free of vested interests. However, there have always been concerns from both within and without the academy as to the appropriateness of counselling and psychotherapy training taking place there (see e.g. the Special Issue of the *European Journal of Psychotherapy & Counselling* on psychotherapy and counselling in the universities: Loewenthal, 2002). The advent of the commodification of education coupled with an increasingly internationally pervasive audit culture (see e.g. Loewenthal, 2010a) together with – in, for example, the UK – the further effect of government policy on psychotherapy and counselling of the Layard report (2005) and the National Institute for Clinical Excellence [NICE] (2009), have increasingly meant that the objectives of the university are becoming synonymous with the state.

The Layard report (2005) can be seen as having two great successes: the first is to convincingly put the case for the talking therapies when previously medication would have been prescribed and the second is to have also persuaded the government that mental health needs to be treated on a population basis. The first is a great achievement but with regard to the second, such population-based medicine is still very much lacking in the provision of treatment of physical health. Yet bringing it in for mental health not only gives the government a central role but it also still focuses on the training of individual psychological therapists in providing what is seen as the best (though for some very narrow and ill-informed) evidence-based practice. This is rather than looking at the causes of mental illness which, ordinarily, a population-based focus would provide also in terms of primary, secondary and tertiary preventative health and social interventions.

We, thus, have counselling and psychotherapy increasingly dominated by government, which in the UK is through the Department of Health. Perhaps in a

1 This section of the chapter is developed from Loewenthal, D. (2013). The unfortunate need for critical psychotherapy and counselling. *European Journal of Psychotherapy & Counselling, 15*(1), 1–4.

similar way to psychology emerging out of philosophy with the claim that rather than having the different viewpoints of philosophers, psychology through science would provide the answer, a similar process is underway with randomised control trials (RCTs) being used in an attempt to finally demonstrate what is the best approach to counselling and psychotherapy. Yet, an examination of the appropriateness of RCTs for determining effective psychological therapeutic approaches with their multi-variable nature shows that scientifically they are non-starters. Surely it will be with incredulity that future generations will look back at such august bodies as NICE prophesying on their basis (see, for example Loewenthal, 2020b).

Psychotherapy and counselling can be seen to necessarily be fundamentally subversive and it seems unlikely that the Department of Health will produce quality assurance criteria to ensure that it is safeguarded, as I have written similarly previously (Loewenthal, 2008, p. 85):

> Jean Laplanche speaks of starting a session with a young person with the words '... your parents want this, but we don't care, we will talk of other things, of whatever you want' (Laplanche, 1992, p. 6). I am taking this to represent a place where psychotherapists and counsellors work – in areas that our society does not want to think about. So, the work of therapy and therapeutic organisations involves holding a paradox. But then what happens to this space if the state wants to regulate it?

There have already been moves to introduce critical counselling and psychotherapy, for example, Feltham (2010) has put the case for the importance of critical thinking in psychotherapy and counselling. There is much to learn also from critical psychiatry and a useful history of it can be found in Thomas and Bracken (2004). Furthermore, there is an important work currently being written, though less directly in the academy still involved with psychotherapy and counselling, for example, on how the construction of the *Diagnostic and Statistical Manual of Mental Disorders* is not based on what most scientists would call science (Davies, 2013). Critical psychology and in particular the work of Ian Parker and colleagues (see e.g. Parker, 1999) has much for us to learn from.

With the aforementioned commodification of education and the increasingly dominant role of the state in determining what counselling and psychotherapy is provided for publicly, there are two further important effects. Firstly, the trainings are now, at least in the UK, increasingly coming with university degrees in counselling and psychotherapy; and particularly in counselling psychology, the students are hoping to get publically funded careers. Secondly, the public is being influenced to increasingly seek out, at least in the first instance, such evidence-based approaches in private practices. There has consequently been a mad scramble for most approaches and professional bodies to show that they too meet these evidence-based criteria, the consequence of which is that there is even less space for questioning and thoughtfulness. Thus, whilst it may have been the hope that universities would provide such a place of enquiry, what has happened is beyond that has always been the danger when one approach dominates an institution. Instead, a cycle has emerged whereby young people interested in psychotherapy and counselling are advised to have an A level biology so that they will eventually have a degree that will give them a job. This is coupled with what would appear to be a shift (see Loewenthal, 2010b) in counselling and psychotherapy from university departments of education (which had previously been very much influenced regarding learning by those such as Carl Rogers) to psychology departments increasingly dominating the psychological therapies (including their very name!). Psychotherapy may, for the time being, still have some play in English and sociology departments but, generally, we can no longer rely on universities serving us as a place, which would encourage thoughts to come to us other than from vested interests. It is thus, with regret, that it would appear that there is an urgent, unfortunate, need for critical counselling and psychotherapy.

There remains the general question though of how European counsellors' and psychotherapists' and their clients'/patients' self-image and coping strategies will be affected by universities being increasingly involved with the state's agenda for our mental health and the extent of the effect of this on our thoughtfulness individually and culturally.

## Altermodernity and the psychological therapies[2]

It's 3.30 in the morning and I'm walking down a tree-lined, well-paved road to a bus stop. Soon after arriving I hear voices and deliberate noises from dustbins and metal railings being hit coming from a side road that links an area of social housing. The noises get louder; there is nobody else around. I decide to walk on quickly to the next bus stop even though I know I might miss the bus and consequently my flight. If only I had avoided all this by taking a recommended taxi to the airport.

Increasingly, people I know take taxis to and from airports even though there are often inexpensive public transport options. Yet, what is seen as the collective good (e.g. public transport, health, education, equality in the provision and pricing of postal and utility services) by some, can be seen as being detrimental to constituent groups and individuals. The 2014 elections for the European Parliament show a revolt against a European Union with nationalistic, and often seen as racist, parties such as Farage's UKIP in the UK and Le Pen's Front National in France getting more votes than any other (27.5% for UKIP, 25% for the Front National). Indeed, they both came first in the 2019 European elections (with the new Farage Brexit Party obtaining 31.6% and the Le Pen's National Rally 23.5%). The reasons for this development are surely manifold and include I imagine those working-class youths that I feared might attack me being without jobs or much education, while those who have recently preached to them the necessity for austerity have seen their house prices rise substantially. What is for certain is that following measures to combat the economic crisis the recovery is uneven, and we are seeing in Europe (Hutton, 2014), as in the USA, further and lasting effects of a 'dramatic rise in income inequality' (Saez, 2013, p. 3).

2 This section of this chapter is developed from Loewenthal, D. (2014). Altermodernity and the psychological therapies. *European Journal of Psychotherapy & Counselling*, *16*(3), 1–4.

Where are European psychotherapists and counsellors in all this? To what extent are the psychological therapies primarily promoting individualism over collectivism? What part, if any, do psychotherapists and counsellors play in the encouragement of individualism and autonomy over collectivism and heteronomy? How many therapists question their paying clients about the misery these clients may have caused others emotionally and economically? Could we, should we, consider facilitating the emotional learning of all for all? What, for example, do we say if our clients complain of too many strangers/immigrants?

I was on my way to Thessaloniki in Greece, a place I look forward to going to not least because of the hospitality of its people (I got the public bus from the airport!). I was there to convene a European meeting on the use of photographs in the emotional learning of prisoners in Europe. Unusually I stayed on after my meetings and went to two museums. The first was the well-known Byzantine Museum where those I was with pointed out a statement from someone who was almost my namesake.

'The past is a foreign country, where we come from' (Lowenthal, 1985, p. 4). Haven't so often those who hold the most extreme views appeared to have been driven by unconscious anxieties as to their own purity?

The second museum I visited was mentioned in the hotel list of museums though the friendly hotel staff said they did not know of it. It was the Jewish Museum. Thessaloniki had once welcomed the Sephardic Jews expelled from Spain in 1492. At one point they became the main population of the city. Yet, the Nazis had managed to exterminate 97.25% of them after first publicly humiliating all the men, imprisoning them and demanding a huge ransom for their release (Mazower, 2005). The university was subsequently built on the Jewish cemetery (that had had over 500,000 graves). Similarly, liberal Greeks I subsequently spoke to still did not appear to want to know of the museum. It was as if what had happened was so terrible no one wanted to know what had happened and potentially their part in it. Worse, when I asked why the museum had a telephone box/sentry type structure built outside of it yet part of the structure, I was told it was so the police could protect the building. In Greece, there was high unemployment with 65% of those between 20 and 30. It is to their credit that it feels relatively safe there and the ultra-right Golden Dawn party, while then coming third, has only 9.4% of the vote. Yet wasn't high unemployment one of the factors that led to Nazism and surely very few of us would want another European World War to make us come to our communal, more worldly, senses?

So what of our future and do we require new conceptual language to really consider it? According to Audouin (2013), the French economist Attali (2013) claims :

> ... there are seven visions of the future which are now vying to become the reality of tomorrow. The first is the hypermodernity, which is measured by its degree of artificiality, and is the extension of the market itself irrigated by an accelerated pace of technical inventions. The second is the amodernity, the fact to simply not think about the future, to be taken by the tyranny of the short-term, which leads to the hypermodernity. The third is retromodernity, a reactionary trend of simply wanting the future as the past. The fourth is ethnomodernity and is the culmination

> of communitarianism and the logic of identities that could, if combined with retromodernity, lead to a fifth, theomodernity, by far the least desirable. The sixth is ecomodernity, whose core values are frugality and carbon sobriety. This way is meaningful, but if society is actually going to implement the changes necessary to stabilize the climate, that is to say, a lifestyle consuming 90% less energy, it cannot get there without a dictatorship, which is not desirable. Fortunately, there is one last vision. This is altermodernity or modernity of altruism. This is in my opinion the only viable long-term modernity, one that makes the happiness of the other the condition of one's own. If this new modernity is needed, being individualistic will soon no longer mean being modern.

Now Nigel Farage has made it clear he doesn't want to be identified with what he considers the racist policies of Marine Le Pen. Yet, this is far from clear for those who vote for him. Isn't it possibly the same for psychological therapists whom I assume would want to be disassociated with any form of racism (aside from their often hatred of other trainings!), yet in encouraging assertiveness, autonomy and generally individualism can't this reinforce our racism – retromodernity rather than altermodernity?

What are the implications then for a European journal where there is an increasing and substantial number of the electorate against the notion of a United Europe? As a European journal, indeed perhaps derived from particularly a mixture of Greek and Hebraic cultures, what should our values be? Should it be to give more space to xenophobic views showing how these are only 'natural' or should it be to claim that our civilisation is one that constantly has to struggle to show that we have to go outwards to welcome the stranger (with always the danger that the second, altermodernity, is a cover for the first, hypermodernity)? To do so means we would need to be more aware of our economic system, yet we seem to suppress and repress this, both as people who are psychological therapists and how we respond to our clients/patients. In the meantime, we perhaps need to understand how threatened we can become when we are even less able to manage our destiny and how xenophobic calls can be stronger than those for brotherly love.

Importantly, this doesn't need to automatically mean that we have immediately to let every stranger who wants to live in any country of their choice do so; or, that the main therapy we provide is within amodernity in order to help us not think about the future.

Yet, what chance is there of altermodernity if 'our natural instinct for altruism is being destroyed by the demands of modern life'. This quote is from a review (McVeigh, 2014) of a recently published book by psychotherapist Music (2014) on how social changes (including consumerism) and the shift towards an ever more unequal society are making us cold-hearted and mean (hypermodernity). In his book, Music points to a series of experiments when a group of toddlers are faced with a situation where an adult pretends to need help:

> The toddlers love helping, they get an intrinsic reward just from the act, until they start to be rewarded for that behaviour with a toy. The group of toddlers rewarded 'extrinsically'– that is, with a toy – quickly lost interest

> in helping. The unrewarded children – who don't know the other group is getting rewards – keep on helping, content with no ulterior reason other than the act of helping.
>
> (McVeigh, 2014)

Isn't this altermodernity in action? Shouldn't we then as psychological therapists help the child (see House & Loewenthal, 2009) be able to stay, and the adult return to being, 'content with no ulterior reason other than the act of helping?'

## Dracula, G8 and the training of critical psychotherapists and counsellors – what is the ideology of psychotherapy and counselling?[3]

In order to explore how our ideology as psychotherapists and counsellors may reinforce through our practices the conflicts outlined above, I wish to describe what might be taken as a spoof, a story amongst stories. In Bram Stoker's Dracula the victims are identified by a mark caused by Dracula's embrace (Stoker, 1994). Dracula was someone else who came from Central Europe (besides Freud and Husserl). In Europe and elsewhere, is there also a consistent mark left on trainees and through them their clients/patients?

I once saw a mark on a French provincial town wall; it read 'G8 ASSASSINS'. This reflects concern that the rich countries of the world meet in order to sustain and enhance their position in *relation* to the 'third world', which we are being asked to refer to as 'less economically developed countries'. Within these eight rich countries there is also a *relational* economic pecking order that has been called a class system. All these countries also have psychological therapists and psychotherapists examining their *relationships* with their clients in order to help these clients with their *relationships* with others. What connection, if any, is there between these macro and micro situations?

If one accepts that the privileged few, in terms of world economies, are living from the added value generated through the manipulation of third world economies, then is this mirrored both in research and in the consulting room? Through various colonial and postcolonial policies, countries in Europe and North America have been able to generate and preserve an economic advantage for their people over many others.

Have such policies attempted to put their populations' minds at rest through developing an ideology where ideology is a dirty word? For sure, many Europeans and North Americans would reach into their pockets if they were to meet for more than a fleeting moment a young child making, for example, sports shoes for us Europeans; but then would our economy as we know it collapse? Yet the mark-up from such products allows that we, the purchasers, gain both the shoes and a well-heeled system.

What then of the relationship between therapist and client/patient – is it not a microcosm of the global economy? Is not therapy also to do with maintaining and enhancing privilege through a form of Dracula-like blood sucking where,

3 This section of this chapter is developed from Loewenthal, D. (2001). Dracula, G8 and the training of psychotherapists and counsellors. *European Journal of Psychotherapy & Counselling, 4*(2), 171–174.

for example, the client is taught the ever-changing cultural forms of seduction within our own social order and its attempt at dominance over other economies? For the behaviourist, conceptually, 'demand' was the buzzword: would one be assertive enough to take one's shoes back to the shop and get them changed, without really much notion of the shop assistant as 'other'? The humanists seemed more interested in need, where the individual primarily puts him- or herself first as the subject with the associated danger of putting the other second as object.

Furthermore, is the analyst's interest in, for example, wishes or desire any less selfish? Deleuze and Guattari (1977) describe various ways in which the seductions of power, status and money encourage the repression of non-conforming revolutionary desire. Deleuze and Guattari oppose themselves to the Freudian and Lacanian emphases on Oedipus and signifier, and therefore the psychoanalytic priesthood. (It is perhaps to be expected that such texts seem to rarely appear in psychological therapy training.) Psychotherapeutic researchers continue to make political choices without necessarily being aware that all the time there is a translation or mediation of something between the researched and the culture we are in. Perhaps one aspect influencing the fashions of and in schools of psychological therapy (and not given the attention it perhaps deserves) is that change is required when the manipulative elements of the current dominant schools become overt. In all these systems of thought, and for any management ideology, is a manipulative seduction essential? People are taught to show that they appear to listen, but if they were really to listen they would be brought face to face with the potential exploitation in their relationships; or in their societies, and in that third world child making those shoes. What is fostered instead is a way of thinking where an examination of the way we think politically throughout our society, including conducting research, is taboo.

There are a few examinations of politics and social responsibility in the therapies, of which Samuels (2001) is an erudite example. It can be argued that these attempts are continually necessary, for, as with the drops of blood at the end of those Dracula films, everyone knows that this means that the monster within has not been eradicated but only suppressed, and needs always to be fought again. Indeed, it may be considered too grandiose a thought for what we as psychological therapists can do (if it did not have the further backing of Deleuze and Guattari); for it was an operation launched from a 'lunatic asylum' (a place familiar to many of us) that 'destroyed' Count Dracula. Deleuze and Guattari stress the collective nature of desire, with 'no separation between the personal and the social, the individual and the collective' (Sarup, 1993, p. 93). Following Reich's interest in the mass psychology of fascism they believe that 'the unconscious is a political force and that fascism dwells in it as much as on the historical stage or in political parties' (Sarup, 1993, p. 93). Deleuze and Guattari argue that there are two types of desire: the paranoid (a reactionary desire – based on the authoritative structure of the hierarchical state) and the schizophrenic (a real desire – centred on flight). These correspond respectively, in social terms, to: the authoritarian (insistence on centralised power) and the libertarian (loose organisations without territorial limits or a system of hierarchy). For Deleuze and Guattari, Freudian psychoanalysis is an example of interpretation as impoverishment. It is when a patient's life has been rewritten according to the terms of Freud's family romance. Yet our students rarely seem permitted to consider such far-reaching alternatives. There is thus less chance that we can fight and leave a different mark, even if only for a while. Or is such talk just a minor safety valve in the process of globalisation creating the illusion of free speech?

So ends this story. What has been presented is not typical of therapeutic training. Similarly, the main streams of research (as well as psychoanalysis, counselling, psychotherapy, psychology and psychiatry) lack much in the way of radical ideological challenges. It would thus appear that students of the psychological therapies learn little about politics and ideology through their formal training. Whilst it is widely acknowledged that this lack of radicalised modernism is apparent in all forms of cultural practice (Lyotard, 1984; Parker, 1997), it is, interestingly, particularly pronounced in the psychological therapies.

Instead might we examine, for example, the following set of questions for psychological therapists (following from the work of a photographer) concerning the encouragement of 'tradition and continuity rather than rupture and change' (Bolton, 1989, p. xiv). Related questions include: How, individually and particularly collectively, do we orchestrate meaning? What other ways of understanding have been dismantled and destroyed? With the success of late modernism, has the political basis of modernism been pushed aside so that we think of our practice as apolitical? Has modernism therefore re-structured knowledge? And what effects have our classification systems and psychological therapistisation processes had on meaning?

Mainstream psychological therapy literature appears apolitical. Where change for the individual is examined, the social consequences in terms of notions of how we view 'the good', 'health' or 'madness', let alone changing fashions in research and the legitimisation of knowledge, are not left open to close scrutiny for long. How is psychotherapy and counselling used to promote class, and national interests? Do claims of lifting repression lift off the chains of oppression or do they become part of a more sophisticated oppression? Mainstream psychological therapy practice appears to offer little by way of analysis of the effects of power in representation, generally encouraging the reverse and implying that what is discussed (in the consulting room) is neutral and above ideology. This tendency is expressed in the frequent refusal of psychological therapy to consider anything other than to incorporate all that is said into an uncritical history of psychotherapy (which is self-contained, self-referential and self-justifying). This potentially strengthens the role of psychotherapy and psychological therapy as the voice for the status quo. Furthermore, there is now the hope, indirectly supported by governments, that the teaching of research will strengthen such professions. So where are the critical histories of psychological therapy; and what place will the psychotherapist/counsellor take up?

What then are the politics of the psychological therapy truth(s)? Danto (1998) uses archival and oral history in attempting to show that Freud proposed the creation of clinics providing free treatment. We could, for example, ask, 'What is the importance of this appearing, opening up what is claimed to be a "little known aspect of the history of psychoanalysis" in terms of changes in the economics of private practice?' In fact, does research of any therapeutic truth require in turn an analysis of power, which in turn depends upon our understanding of the social and political aims of the psychological therapies? Thus, for example, the expectation of what is psychological therapy in itself confines psychotherapy into a particular discursive space. There again, what are the effects of notions of liberalism and objectivity on psychotherapeutic practice? Can they actually supplement social activism and, if so, is this a legitimate aim? To raise such questions is to call into question the ideological closure that would appear to generally characterise psychological therapy training and research.

To choose a final example from Bolton's book on photography (from which most of the above questions are taken), psychotherapy and counselling can be used to honour or repress its subjects, to either complement the '"ceremonial presentation of the bourgeois self" or "establish and delimit the terrain of the other" ' (p. xvii). In this way therapy can be seen to aid in 'the construction of social and moral hierarchies' (p. xvii). Derrida (1996) has argued how the concept of the archive is fundamental to our understanding of meaning. Yet can such developments find their way into our psychological therapy programmes?

The questions raised here, to borrow from Bolton yet again, are 'intended to be productive rather than exhaustive' (p. xv). Behind the above questions is perhaps a whole further set of assumptions, arguments for change in the psychological therapies and for change in the history of history and interpretation of interpretations, arguments for acknowledging the changing relationships within society. Is it too grandiose to consider how critical psychotherapy and counselling can best change society? Is it something that just happens? In other words, do we simply accept the attempted separation of culture and society promoted by late modernism? Perhaps the most important question is why (with the possible exception of sexual difference) such questions have so seldom explicitly been researched?

## Conclusion: 'Our problems originate less in our minds but more reside in the society of which we are a part'

This chapter has started to examine some implications of critical psychotherapy and counselling for the psychological therapies in the twenty-first century. Critical psychotherapy and counselling has been put forward as a possible way of exploring what, for example, the implications are of claims of the death of God, science and the subject for how we research human experience in the clinical encounter? It has been argued that, despite criticisms, it may be essential that the implications of critical psychotherapy and counselling are considered for all existing (modern) modalities of therapy. Through such critical psychotherapy and counselling, such questions arise as to: What is the place of psychotherapeutic theory in examining how we research human experience through psychotherapeutic discourse? Is it possible to have both justice and action? Are, for example, behavioural, humanistic, existential and most psychoanalytic theories merely perpetuating unintentional violence? Has traditional thinking been replaced by theories with fields of knowledge, territories and ownership of psychotherapeutic subject disciplines policed by economic licensing arrangements, which in turn attempt to control language and thought – appropriating difference in the name of difference? How can we research human experience within the context of the clinical encounter in terms of ideas of truth, justice and responsibility? Is there an ethical basis on which we can assist as psychotherapists and counsellors in an embodied way so that we help others not to do violence to others? Indeed, is it possible for therapists, social constructionists, et al not to interrupt their own and others' continuity, not to play roles in which they no longer recognise themselves and whereby they portray not only their commitments but their own substance? A critical psychotherapy and counselling exploration of the above questions in terms of relational ontologies still has to be developed and perhaps this will be made through those such as Derrida, Lacan and in particular Levinas's injunction to put the other first and be responsible for the other's responsibility.

In another sense, this chapter is arguing for the development of psycho-social therapists, and argues that whatever the cultural changes we are currently in, that critical psychotherapy and counselling may be a useful (and even perhaps necessary) way of thinking about starting with practice and the relational. How can we research 'what is' and phenomenologically open up aspects of psychoanalysis such as the unconscious and aspects of post-modernism, which have in part been built on phenomenology? We are subject to these cultural views, yet human agency is possible and can be enhanced, but not if we think we can be fully in charge, nor if we think we are completely subject to aspects such as language.

Critical psychotherapy and counselling may help us to be more thoughtful in and about our practice. For example, being cast into the role of the psychological therapist could be a self-deceptive language. One imagines one is concerned about the other person. Where we want to appear concerned we set up the stage (Gans, 1989) to look like the good psychological therapist – but do we really acknowledge the other? Also, in our attempts for such agency is the potency and potentiality of our own lives diminished? Furthermore, how do we prepare psycho-social therapists for putting the other first, in a way that is not about self/psychological therapist image and privilege? How do we know when they are ready? Perhaps, a Levinasian implication would be to aim towards (as with issues of psychological therapist ethics) not determining our responsibility as teachers of critical psychotherapy and counselling for our trainee's responsibility to those they provide psycho-social therapy, by application of a set of rules. Instead of being primarily concerned with systems of power and knowledge, we should be more concerned with justice on a case by case basis – for real justice cannot be appropriated or territorialised – the therapist has to be just in the moment with another. Such justice may enable us more to explore the 'what is' and not end up being driven by an unthinking cultural (often technical) response. Levinas shows us one way in which we might examine the 'what is', which is influenced by our changing cultural practices, bringing about different fashions in theories and research methods. Critical psychotherapy, in also including the possibility of such aspects as the unconscious and developments in structural linguistics, shows that our way of thinking is inevitably caught up with our socio-cultural setting, but that relational research of aspects of human agency, which we can never fully be in charge of, is, as both Kierkegaard (for existentialism) and Derrida (for post-modernism) have pointed out, more than enough to make us 'tremble'.

Yet, I fear my above emphasis is still too much on psychology and letting in other ideological psycho-social perspectives, not helped by my tendency to use the recently promoted term 'psychological therapist' as a shorthand for psychotherapist, counsellor, psychoanalyst, psychologist, arts and play therapist. This is very different to what might be even a psycho-social therapist let alone a community therapist. As I have written (Loewenthal, 2020a):

> In contrast to Levinas, whom I am in danger here of relying on too much, it may be important for the therapist to have had their own personal exploration of what has been termed 'the hermeneutics of suspicion'(Ricoeur 1970). Here, critical existential-analytic therapists, in order to be able to explore existential concerns, may also have considered: their own potential sexualities and violence (through Freud et al); their own ideological ensnarements (through Marx et al); and, their own values and moralities (through Nietzsche et al).

Critical therapeutic practices, then, by starting with what emerges between two people, may provide the opportunity for us to reconsider how relationships are constructed between ourselves (and eventually between countries), and to consider anew how our theories and practices may serve as a help or a hindrance.

To conclude, hopefully some further examples have been given in this chapter where we can move 'beyond the therapeutic state' to consider and act on the large extent to which 'Our problems originate less in our minds but more reside in the society of which we are a part'.

## References


Attali, J. (2013). *Histoire de la Modernité: comment l'humanité pense son avenir [History of Modernity: how humanity is thinking its future]*. Paris: Éditions Robert Laffont.

Audouin, A. (2013). Interview de Jacques Attali: pour une modernité de l'altruisme. (Betty Bertrand, Trans.). Retrieved June 3, 2014, from www.ressource0.com/interview-de-jacques-attali-pour-une-modernite-de-laltruisme/

Bolton, R. (1989). *The contest of meaning*. Cambridge, MA: MIT Press.

Brooker, A., Canete, M., Dada, M., Hughes, E., Lawrence, S., Loewenthal, D., Mason, J., & Parsloe, S. (2017) Reflections on the first year of a critical psychotherapy supervision collective. *Self & Society*, *45*(1), 63–68.

Danto, A. (1998). The ambulatorium: Freud's free clinic in Vienna. *International Journal of Psychoanalysis*, *79*, 287–300.

Davies, J. (2013). *Cracked: The unhappy truth about psychiatry*. London: Icon Books.

Deleuze, G., & Guattari, F. (1977). *Anti-Oedipus: Capitalism and schizophrenia*. Minneapolis, MN: University of Minnesota Press.

Derrida, J. (1978). *Writing and difference*. London: Routledge and Kegan Paul.

Derrida, J. (1996). *Archive fever*. Chicago: The University of Chicago Press.

Feltham, C. (2010). *Critical thinking in counselling and psychotherapy*. London: Sage.

Gans, S. (1989). Levinas and Pontalis. In R. Bernasconi & S. Wood (Eds.), *The provocation of Levinas: Rethinking the other* (pp. 83-90). London: Routledge.

House, R., & Loewenthal, D. (Eds.). (2009). *Childhood, well-being and a therapeutic ethos*. London: Karnac.

Husserl, E. (1960). *Cartesian meditation: An introduction to phenomenology* (Trans. D. Cairns). The Hague: Martinus Nijhoff.

Hutton, W. (2014). Britain is scared to face the real issue – It's all about inequality. *The Guardian* [online]. Retrieved from www.theguardian.com/commentisfree/2014/jan/19/inequality-threat-recovery-poverty-pay

Kernberg, O. F. (1996). Thirty methods to destroy the creativity of psychoanalytic candidates. *International Journal of Psycho-Analysis*, *77*, 1031–1040.

Kierkegaard, S. (1944). *Concluding unscientific postscript* (Trans D. Swenson). Princeton, NJ: Princeton University Press.

Lacan, J. (1966). *Ecrits*. Paris: Éditions du Seuil.

Laplanche, J. (1992). Notes on afterwardsness. In J. Fletcher & M. Stanton (Eds.), *Jean Laplanche: Seduction, translation and the drives* (Trans. M. Stanton) (pp. 217–223). London: Institute of Contemporary Arts.

Layard, R. (2005). *Mental health: Britain's biggest social problem?* Paper presented at the No. 10 Strategy Unit Seminar on Mental Health, LSE, 20 January 2005. Retrieved December 31, 2012, from www.cep.lse.ac.uk/textonly/research/mentalhealth/RL414d.pdf

Levinas, E. (1969). *Totality and infinity*. Pittsburgh, PA: Duquesne University Press.

Levinas, E. (1985). *Ethics and infinity. Conversations with Philippe Nemo* (Trans. R. Cohen). Pittsburgh, PA: Duquesne University Press.

Levinas, E. (1989). Time and the other. In S. Hand (Ed.), *The Levinas reader* (pp. 37–58). Oxford: Blackwell.

Levinas, E. (1995). Ethics of the infinite. In R. Kearney (Ed.), *States of mind: Dialogues with contemporary thinkers on the European mind* (pp. 177–1999). Manchester: Manchester University Press.

Loewenthal, D. (2001). Dracula, G8 and the training of psychotherapists and counsellors. *European Journal of Psychotherapy & Counselling*, *4*(2), 171–174.

Loewenthal, D. (2002). Special issue on counselling and psychotherapy in the universities. *European Journal of Psychotherapy & Counselling*, 5: 329–418.

Loewenthal, D. (2008). Regulation or ethics as the basis of psychoanalytic training. In I. Parker & S. Revelli (Eds.), *Psychoanalytic practice and state regulation* (pp. 85–93). London: Karnac.

Loewenthal, D. (2010a). Audit, audit culture and therapeia: Some implications for well-being with particular reference to children. In C. Moutsou & L. King (Eds.), *Audit cultures: A critical look at 'evidence-based practice' in psychotherapy and beyond* (pp. 75–96). London: Karnac Books.

Loewenthal, D. (2010b). The psychological therapies and research assessment exercises: Have we got the right REF? *European Journal of Psychotherapy & Counselling*, *12*, 287–291.

Loewenthal, D (2011). *Post-existentialism and the psychological therapies: Towards a therapy without foundations*. London: Routledge.

Loewenthal, D. (2013). The unfortunate need for critical psychotherapy and counselling. *European Journal of Psychotherapy & Counselling*, *15*(1), 1–4.

Loewenthal, D. (2014). Altermodernity and the psychological therapies. *European Journal of Psychotherapy & Counselling*, *16*(3), 1–4.

Loewenthal, D (2015). *Critical psychotherapy, psychoanalysis and counselling: Implications for practice*. London: Routledge.

Loewenthal, D (2020a). Questioning existential psychotherapy from some critical existential-analytic moments. In M. Bazzano (Ed.), *Re-visioning existential therapy*. London: Routledge.

Loewenthal, D. (2020b). Therapy as cultural, politically influenced practice. In S. Shamdasani & D. Loewenthal (Eds.), *Towards transcultural histories of psychotherapies*. London: Routledge.

Lowenthal, D. (1985). *The past is a foreign country*. Cambridge: Cambridge University Press.

Lyotard, J. F. (1984). *The post-modern condition: A report on knowledge*. Manchester: Manchester University Press.

Mazower, M. (2005). *Salonica, city of ghosts: Christians, Muslims and Jews 1430–1950*. London: Harper Perennial.

McVeigh, T. (2014). How big-hearted babies turn into selfish monsters. *The Guardian* [online]/ Retrieved June 3, 2014, from www.theguardian.com/lifeandstyle/2014/may/04/how-babies-turn-into-selfish-monsters?INTCMP=ILCNETTXT3487

Music, G. (2014). *The good life: Wellbeing and the new science of altruism, selfishness and immorality*. London: Routledge.

NICE. (2009). *Treatment and management of depression in adults (CG90)*. National Collaborating Centre for Mental Health, published by the British Psychological Society 2010 [online]. Retrieved from www.guidance.nice.org.uk/CG90/Guidance/pdf/English

Parker, I. (1997). *Psychoanalytic culture: Psychoanalytic discourse in Western society*. London: Sage.

Parker, I. (1999). Critical psychology: Critical links. *Annual Review of Critical Psychology*, *1*, 3–18.

Rogers, C. (1967). *A therapist's view of psychotherapy: On becoming a person*. London: Constable.

Saez, E. (2013). Striking it richer: The evolution of top incomes in the United States (Updated with 2012 preliminary estimates). San Francisco, CA. Retrieved June 9, 2014, from http://eml.berkeley.edu/~saez/saez-UStopincomes-2012.pdf

Samuels, A. (2001). *Politics on the couch*. London: Profile Books.

Sarup, M. (1993). *An introductory guide to post-Structuralism and post-modernism*. Hemel Hempstead: Harvester Wheatsheaf.

Stoker, B. (1994). *Dracula*. Harmondsworth: Penguin Books.

Thomas, P., & Bracken, P. (2004). Critical psychiatry in practice. *Advances in Psychiatric Treatment*, *10*, 361–370.

# Index

*Note*: *Italic* page numbers indicate figures.